Rhode Island

THE THIRTEEN COLONIES

Rhode Island

CRAIG A. DOHERTY

KATHERINE M. DOHERTY

Facts On File, Inc.

Rhode Island

Copyright © 2005 by Craig A. Doherty and Katherine M. Doherty

Captions copyright © 2005 by Facts On File, Inc.
Maps and graph copyright © 2005 by Facts On File, Inc.

Facts On File, Inc.
132 West 31st Street
New York NY 10001

Library of Congress Cataloging-in-Publication Data
Doherty, Craig A.
    Rhode Island / Craig A. Doherty and Katherine M. Doherty.
      p. cm. — (The thirteen colonies)
    Includes bibliographical references and index.
    ISBN 0-8160-5415-0 (hc)
    1. Rhode Island—History—Colonial period, ca. 1600–1775—Juvenile literature. 2. Rhode Island—History—1775–1865—Juvenile literature. I. Doherty, Katherine M. II. Title. III. Series.

    F82.D64 2005
    974.5'02—dc22   2004018100

Text design by Erika K. Arroyo
Cover design by Semadar Megged
Maps and graph by Sholto Ainslie

Printed in the United States of America

VB FOF 10 9 8 7 6 5 4 3 2 1

This book is dedicated to
the many students of all ages
we have worked with and taught over the years.

Contents

Note on Photos

Many of the illustrations and photographs used in this book are old, historical images. The quality of the prints is not always up to current standards, as in some cases the originals are from old or poor-quality negatives or are damaged. The content of the illustrations, however, made their inclusion important despite problems in reproduction.

Introduction

In the 11th century, Vikings from Scandinavia sailed to North America. They explored the Atlantic coast and set up a few small settlements. In Newfoundland and Nova Scotia, Canada, archaeologists have found traces of these settlements. No one knows for sure why they did not establish permanent colonies. It may have been that it was too far away from their homeland. At about the same time, many Scandinavians were involved with raiding and establishing settlements along the coasts of what are now Great Britain and France. This may have offered greater rewards than traveling all the way to North America.

When the western part of the Roman Empire fell in 476, Europe lapsed into a period of almost 1,000 years of war, plague, and hardship. This period of European history is often referred to as the Dark Ages or Middle Ages. Communication between the different parts of Europe was almost nonexistent. If other Europeans knew about the Vikings' explorations westward, they left no record of it. Between the time of Viking exploration and Christopher Columbus's 1492 journey, Europe underwent many changes.

By the 15th century, Europe had experienced many advances. Trade within the area and with the Far East had created prosperity for the governments and many wealthy people. The Catholic Church had become a rich and powerful institution. Although wars would be fought and governments would come and go, the countries of Western Europe had become fairly strong. During this time, Europe rediscovered many of the arts and sciences that had

Vikings explored the Atlantic coast of North America in ships similar to this one. *(National Archives of Canada)*

existed before the fall of Rome. They also learned much from their trade with the Near and Far East. Historians refer to this time as the Renaissance, which means "rebirth."

At this time, some members of the Catholic Church did not like the direction the church was going. People such as Martin Luther and John Calvin spoke out against the church. They soon gained a number of followers who decided that they would protest and form their own churches. The members of these new churches were called Protestants. The movement to establish these new churches is called the Protestant Reformation. It would have a big impact on America as many Protestant groups would leave Europe so they could worship the way they wanted to.

In addition to religious dissent, problems arose with the overland trade routes to the Far East. The Ottoman Turks took control of the lands in the Middle East and disrupted trade. It was at this time that European explorers began trying to find a water route to the Far East. The explorers first sailed around Africa. Then an Italian named Christopher Columbus convinced the king and queen of Spain that it would be shorter to sail west to Asia rather than go around Africa. Most sailors and educated people at the time knew the world was round. However, Columbus made two errors in his calculations. First, he did not realize just how big the Earth is, and second, he did not know that the continents of North and South America blocked a westward route to Asia.

When Columbus made landfall in 1492, he believed that he was in the Indies, as the Far East was called at the time. For a period of time after Columbus, the Spanish controlled the seas and the exploration of what was called the New World. England tried to compete with the Spanish on the high seas, but their ships were no match for the floating fortresses of the Spanish Armada. These heavy ships, known as galleons, ruled the Atlantic.

In 1588, that all changed. A fleet of English ships fought a series of battles in which their smaller but faster and more maneuverable ships finally defeated the Spanish Armada. This opened up the New World to anyone willing to cross the ocean. Portugal, Holland, France, and England all funded voyages of exploration to the New World. In North America, the French explored the far north. The Spanish had already established colonies in what are now Florida, most of the Caribbean, and much of Central and South America. The

Depicted in this painting, Christopher Columbus completed three additional voyages to the Americas after his initial trip in search of a westward route to Asia in 1492. *(Library of Congress, Prints and Photographs Division [LC-USZ62-103980])*

Dutch bought Manhattan and would establish what would become New York, as well as various islands in the Caribbean and lands in South America. The English claimed most of the east coast of North America and set about creating colonies in a variety of ways.

Companies were formed in England and given royal charters to set up colonies. Some of the companies sent out military and trade expeditions to find gold and other riches. They employed men such as John Smith, Bartholomew Gosnold, and others to explore the lands they had been granted. Other companies found groups of Protestants who wanted to leave England and worked out deals that let them establish colonies. No matter what circumstances a colony was established under, the first settlers suffered hardships as

After Columbus's exploration of the Americas, the Spanish controlled the seas, largely because of their galleons, or large, heavy ships, that looked much like this model. *(Library of Congress, Prints and Photographs Division [LC-USZ62-103297])*

they tried to build communities in what to them was a wilderness. They also had to deal with the people who were already there.

Native Americans lived in every corner of the Americas. There were vast and complex civilizations in Central and South America. The city that is now known as Cahokia was located along the Mississippi River in what is today Illinois and may have had as many as 50,000 residents. The people of Cahokia built huge earthen mounds that can still be seen today. There has been a lot of speculation as to the total population of Native Americans in 1492. Some have put the number as high as 40 million people.

Most of the early explorers encountered Native Americans. They often wrote descriptions of them for the people of Europe. They also kidnapped a few of these people, took them back to Europe, and put them on display. Despite the number of Native Americans, the Europeans still claimed the land as their own. The rulers of Europe and the Catholic Church at the time felt they had a right to take any lands they wanted from people who did not share their level of technology and who were not Christians.

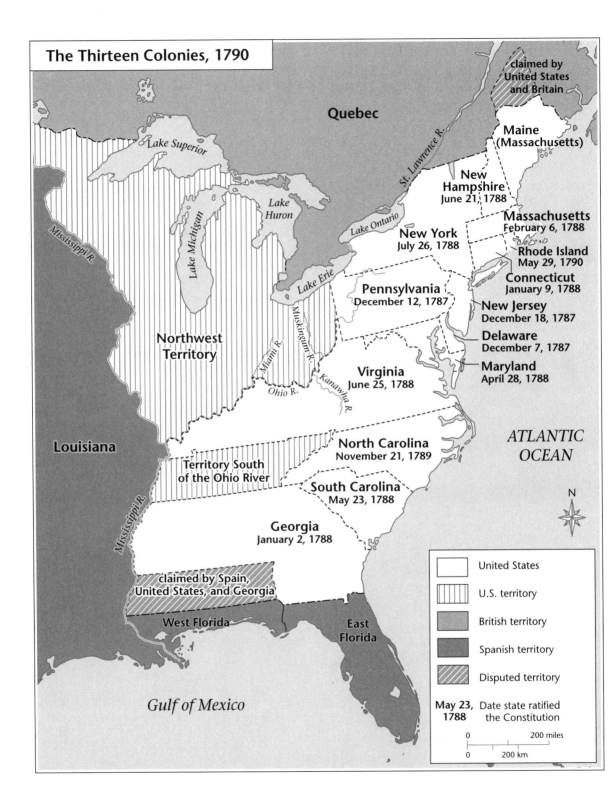

The Thirteen Colonies, 1790

Quebec

Lake Superior

Mississippi R.

Lake Michigan

Lake Huron

Lake Ontario

Lake Erie

Northwest Territory

Louisiana

Muskingum R.

Miami R.

Ohio R.

Kanawha R.

claimed by United States and Britain

Maine (Massachusetts)

New Hampshire
June 21, 1788

St. Lawrence R.

New York
July 26, 1788

Massachusetts
February 6, 1788

Rhode Island
May 29, 1790

Connecticut
January 9, 1788

Pennsylvania
December 12, 1787

New Jersey
December 18, 1787

Delaware
December 7, 1787

Maryland
April 28, 1788

Virginia
June 25, 1788

North Carolina
November 21, 1789

Mississippi R.

Territory South of the Ohio River

South Carolina
May 23, 1788

Georgia
January 2, 1788

claimed by Spain, United States, and Georgia

West Florida

East Florida

ATLANTIC OCEAN

N

Gulf of Mexico

☐ United States

▥ U.S. territory

▧ British territory

▓ Spanish territory

▨ Disputed territory

May 23, 1788 Date state ratified the Constitution

0   200 miles

0   200 km

1

First Contacts

In 1524, Giovanni da Verrazano, an Italian explorer working for the king of France, was the first recorded European visitor to the area that became Rhode Island. He was searching for a passage to Asia, and he reached North America somewhere along what is now the North Carolina coast. He then sailed north looking for a passage to the west. He visited many of the bays along the coast. When Verrazano reached what is now called Narragansett Bay, he was impressed. In his report to the king of France, he described the bay as a place of excellent harbors surrounded by beautiful and fertile land. He also described what is now called Block Island, which lies off the coast, as looking like Rhodes, an island off the coast of Greece. Many believe that this is the source of the name of the colony: Rhode Island.

There may have been other Europeans in Rhode Island before Verrazano, but there is no way to be sure of that. Some have suggested that the Old Stone Mill in Newport, Rhode Island, was built on the ruins of a Viking tower dating back to around 1000 A.D. Although archaeologists are now positive that Vikings settled in Newfoundland and New Brunswick, there is no evidence to prove that they traveled as far south as Rhode Island.

One other possible early visitor to the area was the Portuguese explorer Miguel de Cortereal, who was shipwrecked somewhere along the New England coast in 1502. It is believed that he lived among Native Americans for a number of years. Not

Giovanni da Verrazano sailed to America in 1524 in search of a water route to China. *(National Archives of Canada)*

far from Providence, Rhode Island, in Massachusetts there is a rock that bears an inscription in Latin that says "M. Cortereal 1511 by God's grace the leader of the Indians." No more is known of Cortereal.

After Verrazano, it was 90 years before another European explorer wrote about Rhode Island. Adriaen Block sailed to the mouth of the Hudson River to trade for furs for his Dutch employers. The area that would become New York had been claimed for the Dutch by Henry Hudson in 1609. Block arrived in what the Dutch called New Netherland in 1613. As Block and his crew were preparing to leave, their ship caught fire and sank. They swam to Manhattan Island and, with the help of the Native Americans in the area, were able to build cabins and survive the winter.

They built a small ship called the *Restless* in spring 1614 and explored along the coast to the north. Block claimed much of what is now Connecticut for the Dutch and sailed to Block Island, which is named for him. He also sailed into Narragansett Bay and made contact with the people who lived there. The Native Americans along the bay welcomed and fed Block and his men. Block, and Verrazano before him, found the numerous Native people of the Rhode Island area friendly.

THE NATIVE AMERICANS OF RHODE ISLAND

There may have been as many as 10,000 to 15,000 Native Americans in and around what is now Rhode Island. The borders of these groups were not well defined and often changed as the tribes in the area fought against each other. The Narragansett, Wampanoag, Nipmuc, Niantic, Pequot, and Mohegan all had villages in different parts of Rhode Island. All of these groups spoke dialects of Algonquian languages and lived in a similar fashion. The Narragansett were the largest group, with a population between 5,000 and 10,000 people. They lived mostly on the western shore of Nar-

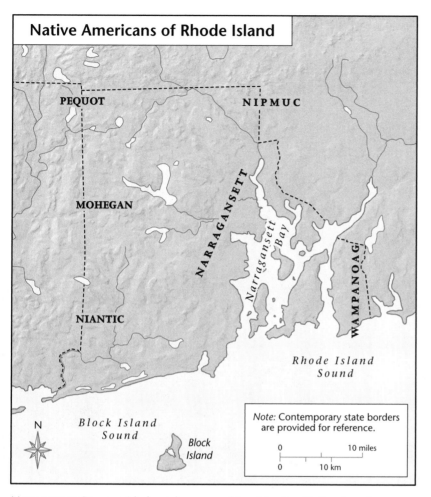

Native Americans of Rhode Island

PEQUOT

NIPMUC

MOHEGAN

NARRAGANSETT

Narragansett Bay

WAMPANOAG

NIANTIC

Rhode Island Sound

N

Block Island Sound

Block Island

Note: Contemporary state borders are provided for reference.

0   10 miles

0   10 km

Narragansett Bay provided a rich source of food for the Native Americans. The area had one of the densest populations of an area north of Mexico.

ragansett Bay. The Wampanoag lived on the eastern side of the bay and eastward into Massachusetts.

The Mohegan and Niantic lived to the south and west of the Narragansett, with most of their settlements in what is now Connecticut. The Nipmuc had lived at the northern end of the bay, but most were forced farther north into Massachusetts by the Narragansett. The Pequot were new arrivals to the area who had migrated to northeastern Connecticut from farther north. Some of their villages were in northwestern Rhode Island. If the population estimates for these tribes are accurate, Rhode Island had one of the densest populations of Native Americans in North America at the time the first English colonies were established.

LIFE IN RHODE ISLAND BEFORE EUROPEAN SETTLEMENT

Although the six different tribes in Rhode Island often fought against each other as the stronger tribes expanded their territory, they all shared a similar lifestyle. Anthropologists refer to the Native Americans of the Northeast as belonging to the cultural group known as Eastern Woodland Indians or as the Northeast

In a late 19th-century engraving published in *Harper's,* some Native Americans relax near their birch-bark wigwams, the type of homes some Eastern Woodland Indians inhabited. *(Library of Congress, Prints and Photographs Division [LC-USZ62-106105])*

Culture Area. All tribes that fall into this category depended on the forests to provide many of their needs. Many of the objects they used on a daily basis were made of wood.

Their houses were called wigwams and were made by arranging saplings (small, flexible trees) in a circle. The tops of the saplings were bent toward the middle of the circle to form a dome. The dome was then covered with bark to keep out the rain. A hole was left at the top of the dome to let out the smoke from the winter cooking fire. In the warmer months of the year, cooking was done outside. Woodland Indians often moved around within their territory to take advantage of seasonally available food and hunting areas. Their most substantial villages were often close to a river or stream that provided fresh water and transportation. They also built walls of logs, known as palisades, around their larger villages to protect themselves from attack.

The people around Narragansett Bay hunted, fished, and gathered wild plants to eat. Deer was the most important animal they hunted. Almost every part of the animal was used. The meat was eaten. The bones and antlers were used for tools. The deerskin was made into clothes. The sinew, the material that surrounds animal muscle, was used like string. In addition to deer, the Indians of Rhode Island harvested many smaller animals and birds. Turkeys were plentiful, as were a number of different types of ducks and geese. The feathers from the various birds were used as decoration on clothing and on headdresses.

Narragansett Bay and the streams that run into it were full of fish and shellfish. The Indians of the area were accomplished fishers who used nets,

Native Americans used almost every part of the white-tailed deer that they killed. *(National Park Service)*

Corn

Corn was first domesticated 6,000 to 8,000 years ago in Central America. Its cultivation spread until it was being grown throughout the temperate regions of North America. Corn is a member of the grass family. Through careful seed selection and hybridization (cross breeding different types of plants) Native Americans were able to develop many varieties of corn and adapt its growth to a wide range of climates. In New England, the Native Americans grew three main varieties of corn. The most important type could be dried and ground into cornmeal to make a variety of dishes. They also grew a variety of corn that was dried whole and added to soups and stews throughout the winter. In addition, it was eaten fresh, like modern corn on the cob. They also grew a variety of corn that was used as popcorn.

Wampum

The Native American groups around Narragansett Bay and throughout the East Coast of North America made beads using clamshells. These beads were known as *wampum,* which comes from the Narragansett word *wampompeag.* They used a variety of clamshells to create white beads, which were always more plentiful than the darker beads. They used parts of the quahog clamshell to produce beads that ranged in color from black to purple and blue. The beads were then strung on leather or hemp twine and fashioned into belts and jewelry.

Much of the wampum was used for decoration, but some wampum belts used a series of symbols that told a story or were used to send messages from one group to another. The Native Americans who had access to the coast often traded wampum for goods with other Native Americans in the interior of the continent.

When Europeans came to the Northeast, they soon began to use wampum as money. In the early years of the American colonies, there was little or no money available. At first, people exchanged food as a form of currency, but this had many drawbacks—the major one being its perishable nature. If the food was not consumed, the person accepting the food would soon lose his or her profit. To solve this problem, the colonists began to accept wampum in exchange for goods, and the colonial governments set exchange rates. They also began to manufacture wampum.

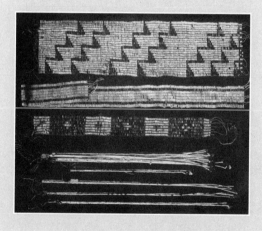

Wampum's uses range from recording agreements to sending messages, but its use as money became more important for Native tribes after the arrival of European explorers and settlers. *(National Archives, Still Picture Records, NWDNS-106-IN-18A)*

spears, hooks and lines, and even their bows and arrows to catch fish. They also made fast, light canoes using the bark of birch trees. They would dry the fish they caught so they could store it for the winter. The shallow waters along the edge of the bay were rich in clams and other shellfish, which were also a source of food. In addition, clamshells were used to make beads that were used for jewelry,

Shamans were integral to the spiritual life and general health of many tribes. In this engraving, an Algonquian shaman prepares for a ritual or ceremony in a Plains Indian style wigwam. *(Library of Congress)*

belts, and for trade with tribes who lived inland. These beads were known as wampum.

In addition to hunting, fishing, and gathering food, the Indians around Narragansett Bay were accomplished farmers who grew corn, beans, and squashes for food. They also grew small amounts of tobacco that was smoked in pipes as part of important religious and social events. Their fields were cleared using fire. When the soil lost its fertility, new fields were cleared. The three main crops they grew were planted in the same fields. The corn would be placed in small hills along with the beans. The two crops helped each other. Beans are able to take nitrogen from the air and add it to the soil. Corn needs a lot of nitrogen to grow. At the same time, the corn provided support for the bean vines. The squash was planted between the corn and bean hills. This made for an efficient use of the land and made it easier to keep their fields free of weeds.

Eastern Woodland Indians also shared a number of social and religious practices. Their religion was based on the idea that all living things were guided by different spirits. They had numerous

Native Americans and Disease

Most scholars agree that the ancestors of the Native Americans originated in Asia and traveled to North America when the two continents were connected by a land bridge between modern-day Siberia and Alaska. During the thousands of years they were isolated from the Asian and European continents, they lost or never developed any immunity to the diseases that the Europeans brought with them to North America.

Common diseases for Europeans like mumps and measles were often fatal for Native Americans. The most deadly disease, which had also killed large numbers of people in Europe, was smallpox. Many of the Wampanoag and other New England tribes were killed by an epidemic brought to the coast of New England by European fishers before the first settlers arrived at Plymouth Rock in 1620. Smallpox epidemics ran through the Native American population of Rhode Island numerous times during the colonial period. Very few Native Americans survived smallpox.

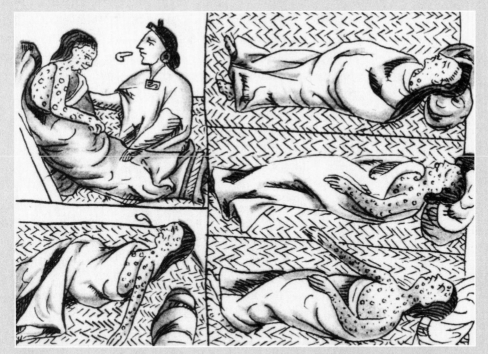

Published in *Historia general de las cosas de Nueva España* in the 1570s, this illustration shows Aztec people sick with smallpox. Native Americans suffered great losses from the influx of European diseases that accompanied colonization. *(Library of Congress)*

ceremonies that were meant to give thanks to various spirits. The Green Corn Festival in summer, when the first corn of the year became ripe, was meant to give tribute to the spirit of the corn. Other festivals were designed to honor different spirits. Before a hunt, the hunters would call on the deer spirit to help them be successful, and when they were, they gave thanks to the spirit. Among the Eastern Woodland Indians, members of the tribe who had special knowledge of the spirit world were known as shamans. They were often responsible for making sure the tribe followed the proper traditions in honoring the spirit world. The shaman might also have special knowledge of herbs and wild plants that could be used to help cure known illnesses.

Families were also important to the Eastern Woodland Indians. They usually lived in groups composed of extended-family members of several generations. When a man married, he became part of his wife's family. Within a tribe, there were usually a number of clans that were often named after birds or animals. Clans are a group of people who share a common ancestor in the distant past. Children became members of their mother's clan. People were not supposed to marry members of their own clan. Among some groups, the marriage ban also included the father's clan.

These extended families often cooperated in hunting, fishing, and gathering. Within the family groups, aunts and uncles often took responsibility for teaching their nieces and nephews the work they would have to do as adults. There was a strong division of labor between men and women. The women often tended the fields, gathered wild plants and herbs, and prepared the food. Men hunted, fished, and became warriors when necessary. However, at busy times of the year, such as during planting, harvesting, or the spring fish runs, the whole group would work together to ensure the survival of the tribe.

Tribes were often led by a single individual known as a sachem. The sachems were chosen based on their wisdom and ability to lead the people, although it was common for the son of a sachem to follow his father as leader. Sachems were almost always men. However, a sachem was not a leader like a president or governor whose laws had to be followed. The sachem was more like a wise person whose advice was often listened to and followed.

With the help of a few other families also in search of religious freedom, Roger Williams established Providence Colony (present-day Rhode Island) on land that he acquired from the Narragansett Indians. *(Library of Congress)*

In each village, there were also leaders who were known as sagamores. They served the village in the same way the sachem served the tribe. They suggested solutions to disagreements between members of the village. They also met in council with the sachem to help make decisions that might affect the whole tribe. In council, everyone was given a chance to speak and a group would keep talking until all the members came to an agreement. Even after this consensus was reached, individual members of the tribe could decide not to go along with the decisions of the sagamores and sachems.

This fact often caused problems between European settlers and the Indians of the area. The colonists would negotiate treaties and land purchases with the sachem and/or the sagamores and then expect everyone in the tribe to go along with the agreement. This was not always the case, and the lack of understanding of how the Native American and European cultures worked often led to serious conflicts between the two groups.

The Indians of the area helped the earliest European settlers survive in North America. Members of the Wampanoag helped the Pilgrims survive at Plymouth Colony, in what is now Massachusetts. Colonists soon learned how to grow Native American crops as well as harvest the abundant marine and animal life of the region, and the Indians adopted firearms, European-style clothing, and metal tools. Unfortunately, the Europeans brought diseases with them from Europe that were unknown in the Americas. Many more Indians died from these diseases than they did in wars with the colonists. Many were also killed as the two sides fought to control the land.

When Roger Williams came from Massachusetts to create a new colony at what would become Providence, Rhode Island, in 1636, he worked hard to have good relations with his Native American neighbors. Williams and those who followed him to Rhode Island dealt fairly with the sachems from the various tribes. The best known sachems were Canonicus and Miantonomi (also spelled Miantonomo) of the Narragansett, Massasoit of the Wampanoag, and Uncas of the Pequot. Unfortunately, the struggling colony of Rhode Island was overshadowed by land-hungry Puritans in Massachusetts and Connecticut, who pursued a policy of forcing Indians to give up their lands. The policies of Rhode Island's neighbors led to war between colonists and Native Americans. Through war and disease, a huge percentage of the Indians of Narragansett Bay were wiped out during the colonial period.

2

First Settlement

When colonists first left England for what was soon called New England, they came for many reasons. Many of the leaders of the first colonies in what is now Massachusetts came for the opportunity to create a place where they could practice their Protestant religion without interference from the Church of England. Others came for the opportunity to escape the strict social structure of England that limited opportunities for many. It was not long before some of the colonists came into conflict with the leadership of the colonies.

William Blackstone moved to the colonies in 1623, first settling in present-day Boston and moving two years later to a spot in present-day Rhode Island. He was the first English settler on the land that would become Rhode Island. *(Library of Congress, Prints and Photographs Division [LC-USZ62-43798])*

The Puritan and Pilgrim leaders wanted the right to practice their religions as they saw fit. However, they had no toleration for people who disagreed with their beliefs. Some who disagreed chose to live in the unsettled areas where no one would bother them. William Blackstone was one of those who wanted to live without interference from others. He arrived in New England in 1623 and decided to build a house on a peninsula known by the local Indians as Shawmut that is now called Beacon Hill in

After many clashes with religious leaders in both Plymouth and Massachusetts Bay Colonies, Roger Williams founded Providence in present-day Rhode Island. *(Library of Congress, Prints and Photographs Division [LC-USZ6-846])*

Boston. When the Puritans arrived in 1630, he invited them to share the excellent spring near his house.

Soon there were many people moving into what they called Boston. Blackstone did not like being crowded by his neighbors. He also disagreed with some of the religious ideas of the Puritans. He decided to once again move to an unsettled area of New England. In 1635, he moved to a spot about 50 miles southwest of Boston, just north of the present-day town of Cumberland, Rhode

Island. He was the first English settler in what would become Rhode Island. However, he really had no interest in being part of any community, and he is not given credit for establishing the colony of Rhode Island and Providence Plantation.

ROGER WILLIAMS AND PROVIDENCE PLANTATION

Most agree that Rhode Island's colonial beginnings came a year later when Roger Williams came to the area and set up a place where everyone, no matter what their religious beliefs, was welcome. Roger Williams and his wife Mary came to Boston in 1631 where he took a job as assistant pastor in the Boston church. Williams quickly found himself in trouble for disagreeing with the Puritan leaders in Boston.

In the Massachusetts Bay Colony, the church and the government were almost the same thing. Someone who disagreed with the church was seen as breaking the law. Those who committed crimes against the laws of the government were seen as committing crimes against God. People who refused to conform to this church-state were treated very harshly. For minor infractions, they might be put in the stocks, a wooden frame that locked a person's arms, legs and/or head in place. The stocks were usually located in the center of town, where people could insult and sometimes throw things at those being punished. It was assumed that this type of public humiliation would force people to behave.

Roger Williams
(ca. 1603–1683)

Roger Williams was born in London, where his father was a successful tailor. His mother came from a well-to-do family, and it is likely that Roger was taught to read and write at home. However, as a teenager he came into conflict with his parents because he had developed some religious views that did not coincide with theirs. Roger took his religious beliefs very seriously and was observed by Sir Edward Coke taking shorthand notes of the sermon in church one Sunday morning. Coke, who was a lawyer, took an interest in Williams and soon had him using his short-hand skills to record court proceedings.

Coke realized that Williams lacked a formal education and arranged for him to attend the Charter House School. From there, Williams won a scholarship to Cambridge where he earned his baccalaureate degree in 1627. In college, Williams further refined his religious ideas, but, due to the intolerance of the times, he remained silent about them so he could complete his education. After college he worked as a private chaplain for a wealthy English family at their country home. In 1629, Williams married Mary Brainard, who was a maid.

At this point, Williams wanted to escape the intolerant social and religious structure of England. He began going to meetings with a group that was interested in becoming part of Massachusetts Bay Colony. John Winthrop, who would become the colony's governor, was part of this group. When Williams agreed to become a part of the Puritan group, he probably did not understand that these people would be as intolerant in their beliefs as the Church of England.

For those who committed more serious wrongs, the Puritans used whippings, mutilations, banishment, and execution as punishment. To avoid the severity of the Boston leaders, Williams moved to Salem, where the leaders were not as strict. He took a job as a teacher at the Salem Church, but when Governor Winthrop complained that Salem could not hire Williams without permission from the government, Williams was forced to move again. This time he went to Plymouth, where the leaders in Boston had no authority.

Since arriving in New England, Williams had taken an interest in the Native Americans of the area. He felt that they were "children of God" and deserved fair treatment. He worked to convert Indians to Christianity and learned to speak their languages. While in Plymouth, he met Massasoit, the sachem of the

Stocks were used in the colonies as a form of punishment. These stocks are a reconstruction at Colonial Williamsburg in Virginia. *(Library of Congress, Prints and Photographs Division [LC-USZ62-97883])*

Wampanoag, and Canonicus, the sachem of the Narragansett. The friendship of the two Indian leaders played a major role in the success of Providence Plantation and Rhode Island.

When Williams became critical of the Plymouth Colony leaders for taking Indian land without paying for it, he was forced to move back to Salem. His criticism of the Puritan leadership increased, and Williams was soon called before the court. In 1634, the court gave him a choice of either admitting his beliefs were wrong or being punished. At first, the people of Salem supported Williams, but the more powerful leaders in

John Winthrop was the first governor of Massachusetts Bay Colony. *(Library of Congress, Prints and Photographs Division [LC-USZ62-124240])*

Boston forced them to abandon Williams. In July 1635, he was again brought before the court, and he still refused to give up his beliefs.

In October 1635, Williams made his third and final appearance before the court in Boston. They gave him one more chance to confess his crimes against the state and sins against the church. Williams would not give in and was told he had 30 days to change his mind or be banished from the colony. At the end of the 30 days, the banishment order went into effect, but Williams was given until spring to leave because his wife was pregnant and he was not well. When people in Salem continued to support him, the leaders in Boston decided they could not wait until spring. On January 11, 1636, John Haynes, the new governor, ordered that Williams be sent back to England.

Again, Williams pleaded that he was not well enough to travel. The next time the Boston officials sent for him, they sent a troop of 14 men to arrest him. Knowing he could not avoid his punishment if he stayed in Salem, Williams left his wife, children, and friends and headed into the wilderness in the middle of the winter. It has been reported that the former governor John Winthrop secretly suggested that Williams move to the area of Narragansett Bay. Whether he was following the advice of Winthrop or knew that his Indian friends would not be as cruel as his English enemies, Williams ended up in Sowams (near present-day Warren, Rhode Island), the winter village of the Wampanoag sachem Massasoit.

When spring came, Williams negotiated with Massasoit for land along the Seekonk River on the east side of the bay. He and five other colonists began to put up houses and plant crops. However, this land was claimed by Plymouth Colony, which did not want trouble with the more numerous Puritans in Massachusetts Bay Colony. The Plymouth colonists told Williams he could not stay in their territory, and he was forced to leave his first attempt at creating a settlement.

He and his handful of followers moved across the bay to where they found an excellent spring. It was near the bay where the Mooshassuc and Pawtuxet streams join. This spot did not have any

Originally published in *Harper's New Monthly Magazine* in 1857, this engraving supposedly depicts Massasoit's home. *(Library of Congress, Prints and Photographs Division [LC-USZ62-96220])*

During John Carver's tenure (1621) as governor of Plymouth Colony, Carver and Massasoit negotiated a treaty that kept peace between the colonists and the Wampanoag for the next 50 years. *(Library of Congress, Prints and Photographs Division [LC-USZ62-96230])*

Indians living on it, but it was claimed by both the Wampanoag and the Narragansett. Williams negotiated a deed with his neighbors that was signed by the sachems Canonicus, Massasoit, and Miantonomi. Williams named his new community Providence, and it became the first permanent colonial settlement in Rhode Island.

THE PEQUOT WAR

In the early days of the colonies, there was a series of wars between the Native Americans in New England and the English settlers. The first of these was the Pequot War. The leaders of Massachusetts were even more intolerant of Native Americans than they were of people like Roger Williams. Because most Native Americans were not Christians, the Puritan leaders felt they had no rights.

As more and more English people arrived in Massachusetts, they were encouraged to spread out up and down the coast. There were soon settlements north into what is now Maine and south into what would become Connecticut. In Connecticut, the settlers quickly moved up the Connecticut River into territory that belonged to the Pequot tribe. Saybrook was established at the mouth of the

Massasoit was grand sachem of the Wampanoag bands. *(Library of Congress, Prints and Photographs Division [LC-USZ62-120508])*

river with a substantial fort. The communities of Wethersfield, Hartford, and Windsor, in what would become Connecticut, and Springfield, in Massachusetts, were all settled along the river without taking into consideration the Pequot who already lived in the area.

At first, the colonists used the Pequot as trading partners. They exchanged cloth and metal objects for furs. However, the Pequot had fought with many of their Native American neighbors to defend their territory before and after the coming of the English. They were not going to let their land be taken without a fight. As more and more settlers moved into Pequot territory, conflict was inevitable.

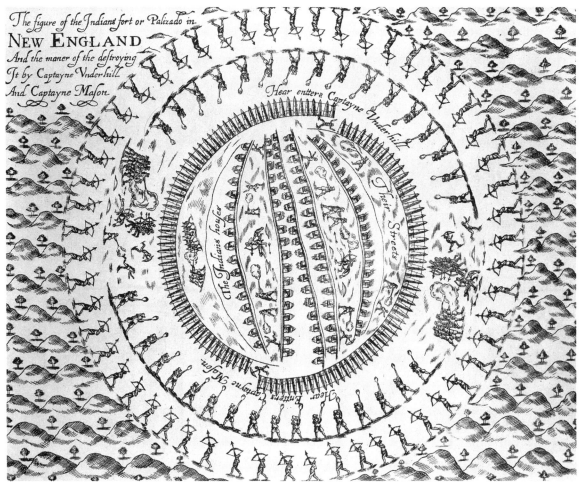

First published in a 1638 book, this illustration depicts the Pequot village that a colonial army led by Captains John Underhill and John Mason attacked in 1637. *(Library of Congress, Prints and Photographs Division [LC-USZ62-32055])*

The first strike in what would become known as the Pequot War is not clearly recorded. The leaders of the Massachusetts Colony considered the death in 1634 of Captain John Stone, a trader of uncertain reputation, as the first strike in the war. Stone was killed by the Western Niantic, who were allies of the Pequot. The leaders of the colony used Stone's death as the reason to force the Pequot to sign a treaty with the colony that was unfavorable to them. Two years later, when another trader, John Oldham, was killed by Native Americans on or near Block Island, off the coast of what became Rhode Island, Massachusetts sent an expedition of 90 men led by John Endecott to get revenge.

It is not known if the Narragansett living on Block Island had anything to do with Oldham's death. Pequot were believed to have hijacked the boat. This did not matter to Endecott's force. They burned a number of Narragansett villages on Block Island and then crossed over to Connecticut to search out any Pequot who had been involved. The colonists at Saybrook were very upset that the force from Massachusetts had been sent to deal with the Pequot. They feared that if the Pequot were attacked by Endecott and his men, they would suffer the reprisals.

Endecott did not listen to the people of Saybrook and attacked several Pequot villages. His troops burned the villages and killed one Native American. Sassacus, the Pequot leader, did as the people of Saybrook feared and sought revenge. In the winter of 1636–37, Sassacus and the Pequot attacked the fort at Saybrook and a number of smaller settlements. In spring 1637, the Pequot attacked Wethersfield and killed nine colonists. Canonicus, the leader of the Narragansett, wanted to join the Pequot as revenge for his people who had been killed on Block Island, but Williams convinced him to help the English instead.

The costs to the Pequot for these attacks were devastating. A large colonial army was gathered under the command of Captains John Underhill and John Mason. In addition to a large force of colonists, many Native Americans joined in. The colonists used the traditional rivalries among the Native American groups to recruit allies. Mohegan, Narragansett, and Niantic warriors fought alongside the colonists. On May 26, 1637, the combined forces attacked Sassacus's village at what is today Mystic, Connecticut. At first, the Pequot were able to repel their attackers from behind their palisades. However, the colonists and their allies set the village on fire. The Pequot who tried to escape were killed. Those who stayed behind died in the flames. Between 500 and 1,000 Pequot, mostly women, children, and old men, died during the battle.

Sassacus and many of his warriors had fled. They were found in July in a swamp west of New Haven and were attacked again. This time when Sassacus escaped, he fled to the territory of the Mohawk. The Mohawk did not want to appear to be on Sassacus's side. They beheaded him and let the colonists know they would no longer have to fear the Pequot leader.

The Pequot who survived were rounded up and became slaves. The colonists gave some of the Pequot to their Native American allies

An expedition led by John Endecott attacked Narragansett villages on Block Island in 1636 during the Pequot War. *(Picture Collection, The Branch Libraries, The New York Public Library, Astor, Lenox and Tilden Foundations)*

as payment for their help. Other Pequot were sold in the slave markets of the Caribbean. A few Pequot avoided capture and escaped. They joined other tribes that were willing to take them in. The colonists had effectively wiped out the Pequot and stopped the use of Pequot tribal and place-names. Almost 20 years later, in 1655, the colonists freed the remaining Pequot slaves in New England and allowed them to return to the site of their village on the Mystic River.

The other tribes around Narragansett Bay were appalled by the treatment of the Pequot. Eventually both the Wampanoag and Narragansett went to war against Massachusetts. By the end of the 17th century, the Native Americans of southern New England had ceased to be a threat to the English colonies.

3

Creating the Colony of Rhode Island

PORTSMOUTH AND NEWPORT

As Roger Williams and his followers worked out the details of life at Providence Plantation, others came to Narragansett Bay to escape the harsh rule of the Pilgrims and Puritans. Anne Hutchinson and her family had come to Boston in 1634 because of their desire to follow the religious teachings of John Cotton. Cotton was one of the Puritans' most famous religious leaders. In Boston, Anne Hutchinson began holding meetings in her home, where people came together to talk about their religious thoughts.

At first, no one saw any harm in this, and they assumed that those involved in the meetings at Hutchinson's believed in all aspects of Puritan doctrine. However, as time went on, and the meetings grew in popularity, Anne Hutchinson and others began to discuss religious ideas that were different from Puritan beliefs. The major points of the disagreement were over the idea of personal salvation. Hutchinson and her followers seemed to be saying that they could find God's grace without the restrictive rules of the Puritan church.

The church was the basis of Puritan society and, therefore, extremely important to the leaders of Massachusetts. Hutchinson was first put on trial in 1637 for speaking against the Puritan ministers. This was not a very serious charge, but the leaders of Massachusetts used the trial as a way to get Hutchinson to talk about

Anne Marbury Hutchinson
(1591–1643)

Anne Marbury Hutchinson was born in 1591 in Alford, England. Her father was a minister and schoolteacher who spoke out against the Church of England and was arrested a number of times for his Puritan beliefs. After Anne married William Hutchinson in 1612, the couple traveled 25 miles on Sundays to Boston, England, to hear the Puritan leader John Cotton preach. When Cotton sailed to Massachusetts in 1632 to join the new Puritan colony there, the Hutchinsons decided to follow a year later. In Boston, Anne Hutchinson began to develop beliefs that went against the ideas of the Puritan leaders of the community. After being convicted of crimes against the Puritan church, Anne moved to Rhode Island with a number of her followers in 1638. After the death of her husband in 1642, Hutchinson made a decision that proved fatal.

She feared that Massachusetts was about to take over Rhode Island and that she would find herself once again banished or in prison. To avoid that fate, she moved with her many children to a farm near the Dutch town of New Amsterdam (modern-day New York City). In 1643, the Dutch governor, William Kieft, ordered an attack on local Indians. In retaliation, numerous outlying farms were attacked, including the Hutchinson farm. Anne Hutchinson and five of her 16 children were killed.

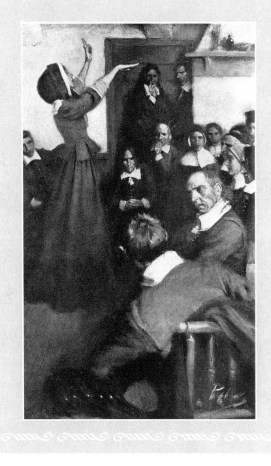

Anne Hutchinson's religious beliefs and practices were challenged in the Massachusetts Bay Colony, from which she was banished. She fled, setting up her colony on Aquidneck Island called Pocasset, with other people seeking religious freedom, but later moved, yet again, to Long Island. *(Library of Congress)*

her beliefs. When questioned about how she came to hold ideas that were contrary to the rules of the Puritans, Hutchinson said that she had experienced a divine revelation. In other words, she had received her ideas directly from God.

The Puritans believed that God had not spoken directly to humans since the Bible chapter known as the Book of Revelation had been written thousands of years ago. As a result of her statements, the court called her an antinomian—someone who disregarded the laws of the church and civil authority. She was charged with heresy and, after another trial, she was excommunicated in March 1638 and told to leave Massachusetts.

By the end of her second trial, Hutchinson had a rather large following. Many feared sharing in her fate and abandoned her ideas. Others followed John Wheelwright, Hutchinson's brother-in-law, who left to start a new community in New Hampshire. The largest group of Hutchinson's followers was led by William Coddington, who had been an important leader in Massachusetts, and John Clarke, a recent arrival in Boston who was upset with the strictness of Puritan society. Clarke and Coddington set out by ship ahead of Hutchinson with a large group of followers. It was their plan to head for the unsettled regions of Delaware Bay to start a new community.

As they headed south, they made a stop at the new community of Providence and met with Roger Williams. Williams convinced them there was no reason to go all the way to Delaware Bay. He

Antinomian Ideas

The word *antinomian* comes from the Greek word *anti*, which means "against," and *nomos*, which means "law." It was originally used in the 1530s by Martin Luther to describe the religious beliefs of the German preacher Johann Agricola. He said that the human laws had no bearing on the salvation of people's souls. Some saw his argument as a way to say that people did not have to obey the law. The Puritan leaders of Massachusetts used the term *antinomian* to describe Hutchinson and her followers because they refused to follow the laws of the church.

suggested that they could just as easily establish their community on Aquidneck Island in Narragansett Bay. When they accepted Williams's idea, the Narragansett leaders Canonicus and Miantonomi came to Providence and agreed to sell Aquidneck Island to Clarke and Coddington. They were to pay for the island with a large amount of wampum.

Clarke and Coddington moved to the island with their followers and began setting up a new community at the north end of the island using the Narragansett name Pocasset. Anne Hutchinson, her husband, their 16 children, and a number of other followers soon arrived in Pocasset. At Hutchinson's suggestion, the name of the community was changed to Portsmouth. Coddington had assumed the position as town leader but soon found himself in opposition to many of Hutchinson's ideas.

Coddington had admired Anne Hutchinson's defiance of the authority in Boston but had not agreed with all her ideas about government. By 1639, the friction between the two groups in

This house, shown in an undated photograph, was built between 1710 and 1715 and is one of the oldest in North Providence, Rhode Island. *(Library of Congress, Prints and Photographs Division [HABS, RI,4-PROVN,1-4])*

William Coddington established Newport, Rhode Island's third town, on the southern tip of Aquidneck Island. This pen-and-ink drawing of Coddington's house in the town was completed before 1886. *(Library of Congress, Prints and Photographs Division [HABS, RI,3-NEWP,16-1])*

Portsmouth had grown and Coddington decided to lead the more moderate members of the community to the southern end of the island and set up Newport, which became Rhode Island's third town established by English settlers. All three towns—Providence, Portsmouth, and Newport—guaranteed people the freedom to

Trinity Church in Newport was built in 1725–26 and has been used ever since as a place of worship. *(Library of Congress, Prints and Photographs Division [HABS, RI,3-NEWP,17-1])*

practice religion as they wanted. Many who could not tolerate the harsh conditions in Massachusetts and Plymouth flocked to the havens along Narragansett Bay.

WARWICK

One new arrival in Portsmouth was Samuel Gorton. Gorton considered himself the "professor of the mysteries of Christ." He had been kicked out of both the Massachusetts and Plymouth colonies for his heretical religious ideas. Not only were his religious ideas unconventional, but he also created discord in the community. Despite the problems he seemed to cause wherever he went, Gorton had attracted a group of followers who were called Gortonists. They did not believe in heaven or hell, nor did they accept the political authority of the colony's community.

After creating a number of problems in Portsmouth, Gorton was forced to move on once again. This time, he went to Providence, probably assuming that the famously tolerant Roger Williams would leave him and his followers alone. After Gorton angered the local leaders, he moved to Pawtuxet, which was still part of Providence but would later become Cranston. The people in Pawtuxet did not want Gorton and his people in their community either. However, they did not get along with the more established group of people in Providence, so they turned to Massachusetts for help in dealing with Gorton. The leaders in Massachusetts were keeping an eye on Providence Plantation and the settlement on Aquidneck Island. They claimed the area was part of their colony.

In fall 1642, the leaders in Pawtuxet asked Massachusetts for help dealing with Gorton. Governor Winthrop issued orders against the Gortonists, who were once more faced with the need to move on. However, they decided it was time to find their own place, where they could live without interference. Gorton negotiated with Miantonomi to buy a large tract of land from the Narragansett south of Providence Plantation. At first, the area went by its Indian name: Shawomet. They quickly moved to the area that is now called Warwick and built houses.

The leaders in Pawtuxet were not satisfied. In part, they were greedy and wanted more land. They also wanted to break the control of Providence. In fall 1643, they once again called upon Massachusetts governor Winthrop to help. This time, they took two Narragansett sagamores who were disgruntled over the land deal that Miantonomi made to Boston. It has been suggested that they were upset because they did not get a share of the 400

Samuel Gorton and his followers, the Gortonists, fled from town to town looking for a place they could live how they wanted. In this 1881 drawing, the Gorton party is under siege. *(Picture Collection, The Branch Libraries, The New York Public Library, Astor, Lenox and Tilden Foundations)*

fathoms (2,400 feet) of wampum Gorton had agreed to pay for Shawomet.

When Governor Winthrop had heard from the sagamores and the representatives of Pawtuxet, he called for Miantonomi and Gorton to appear in Boston. Miantonomi answered the governor's call and felt insulted by the treatment he received in Boston. Gorton had already been mistreated by the narrow-minded leaders of Boston, and he had no intention of going back. Winthrop had other ideas and sent 40 soldiers to Shawomet to get Gorton and his followers.

Some of the people in Shawomet barricaded themselves in a house and fired upon the soldiers. After a few days, the Gortonists gave up after the Massachusetts soldiers promised them safe passage. Gorton and six of his followers were taken to Boston for trial. The others were forced to return to Aquidneck Island for the winter because the soldiers took over their houses and confiscated their animals.

In Boston, Gorton and his six followers were charged with heresy and blasphemy and were quickly convicted and sentenced to death. However, Governor Winthrop reduced their sentences, had them put in chains, and made them work at hard labor for the winter. In spring 1644, they were released on the condition that they leave Massachusetts and not return to Providence or Shawomet. They went and joined the others who had been forced to leave Shawomet for Aquidneck Island.

Roger Williams was concerned by the aggressive actions of Massachusetts and the threat posed by the New England Confederation. In 1643, he returned to England to try and get a separate royal charter for the four English settlements of Providence, Shawomet, Portsmouth, and Newport. When Gorton was released

The New England Confederation
(1643–1684)

While Massachusetts interfered with the situation along Narragansett Bay, its leaders also went to work with the established colonies of Plymouth, New Haven (later part of Connecticut), and Connecticut to create an alliance for defense against the increasing hostility of some of the Native Americans in New England. The alliance, known as the New England Confederation, stayed in existence for more than 40 years. During that time, there was as much dissension among the members as there was cooperation. Massachusetts, because it had the most people, thought it should be in control of the confederation. The other members were concerned that they might lose their independence and resisted. In 1675, the confederation came together to nearly wipe out the Indians of southern New England in what is known as King Philip's War. In 1684, when the political situation in England changed drastically, the Massachusetts charter was revoked and the New England Confederation was ended.

After being approached by Samuel Gorton and Roger Williams, Robert Rich, the earl of Warwick, gave them a patent establishing Providence Plantations as an individual colony. Gorton changed the name of Shawomet to Warwick to show his appreciation. *(Library of Congress, Prints and Photographs Division [LC-USZ62-121204])*

from Massachusetts, he followed Williams to England.

PATENT FOR PROVIDENCE PLANTATIONS

In England, both Williams and Gorton found a sympathetic supporter in Robert Rich, the earl of Warwick, who had been appointed by the government to oversee all of England's colonies around the world. After listening to the two men from Narragansett Bay as well as those who represented Massachusetts Bay Colony, the earl created a document known as the "Patent for Providence Plantations." The patent was approved by Parliament, and Gorton and Williams headed back to Narragansett Bay in 1644.

The name of Shawomet was changed to Warwick to honor the earl. Providence Plantations now was an official English colony made up of Portsmouth, Newport, Providence, and Warwick. The patent gave the people of the colony the right to govern themselves, which also allowed them to continue the ideas of religious tolerance that the colony had been founded on. At least for the moment, the Providence Plantations were safe from the designs of their much larger neighbors. The four towns combined and went about the task of creating a government and increasing the wealth and population of their colony.

At about the same time, the people on Aquidneck decided to change the name of their island. They chose to name it Rhode Island, which would soon replace Providence Plantations as the name of the whole colony. In 1647, representatives of the four towns met for the colony's first general assembly. One of the first actions of the assembly was to choose the simple motto of "Hope" for the new colony. A number of problems would arise in the future for Rhode Island, but during them all, the smallest of the

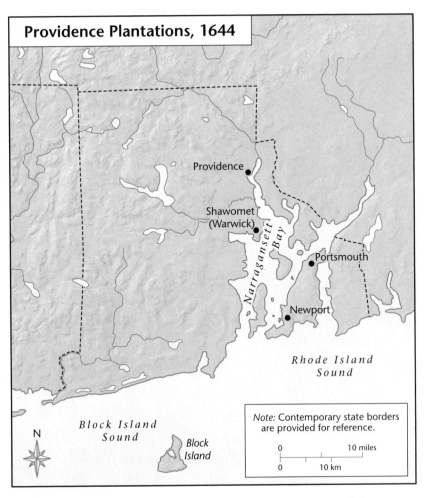

Providence Plantations, 1644

Providence

Shawomet
(Warwick)

Narragansett Bay

Portsmouth

Newport

*Rhode Island
Sound*

*Block Island
Sound*

*Block
Island*

N

Note: Contemporary state borders
are provided for reference.

0   10 miles

0   10 km

In 1644 the king granted a charter to Providence Plantations, and the towns of Providence, Newport, Portsmouth, and Warwick officially became a colony.

American colonies remained a place that attracted and tolerated people with a wide range of religious beliefs from all over the colonies and Europe.

The Growth of Rhode Island

Despite the new motto of "Hope," not everyone in Rhode Island was happy with the progress the colony had made in its first few years. William Coddington wanted his own colony. He went to London in 1648 to claim that he was the owner of Aquidneck Island and the nearby Conanicut Island. He wanted the Crown to recognize his claim and make him governor for life.

Built between 1759 and 1763 and shown here in a 1971 photograph, Touro Synagogue in Newport, Rhode Island, is the oldest synagogue in North America. *(Library of Congress, Prints and Photographs Division [HABS, RI-3NEWP,29-1])*

Although he and a partner would later buy Conanicut Island, at the time he was in London, his claim was based on a lie. The idea of Portsmouth and Newport becoming a separate colony had no support at home. At this time, there was a lot of confusion in England caused by the overthrow of King Charles I by a Puritan revolution in 1649. The government of Oliver Cromwell granted Coddington a charter on April 3, 1651 giving him his two-island colony and making him governor for life. To establish control, the new governor of Rhode Island returned to Newport. Armed men led by John Clarke, who had been with him when they bought Aquidneck Island from the Narragansett, disagreed with Coddington's maneuver and forced him to leave for Massachusetts.

Governor Coddington rushed off to Boston, rather than face his angry neighbors. Clarke and Roger Williams went to London to meet with Oliver Cromwell. Once they had presented the facts, the patent of 1644 was renewed by the Puritan government and the four towns were once again united.

RELIGIOUS HAVEN

Roger Williams, Anne Hutchinson, Samuel Gorton, and many of Rhode Island's other early settlers all came to the colony so they could follow their own religious beliefs. As the people shaped the future of the colony, they had many differences of opinion, but one constant was the idea that all people had the right to follow their own religious beliefs. This religious tolerance attracted people of a wide variety of beliefs to the colony.

In 1639, Roger Williams helped establish the first Baptist church in America. In 1657, a group of Quakers arrived on Aquidneck Island from Massachusetts and Connecticut, where the treatment of Quakers had been extremely harsh. Massachusetts had gone as far as executing some Quakers because of their beliefs. Until Quaker settlements were established in New Jersey and William Penn was granted the colony of Pennsylvania to be a refuge for Quakers, Rhode Island was one of the few places Quakers were welcomed.

The Society of Friends, also known as Quakers, traces it roots to George Fox's preaching about an "inner light" that all people have. Fox claimed it was the manifestation of Christ in each person. This early 19th-century watercolor shows a traveler's interpretation of a Quaker. *(National Archives of Canada)*

Quakers

The first half of the 17th century was a time of religious upheaval in England. Many people were upset with the official church, known as the Church of England. The Pilgrims who came to Plymouth Colony were called separatists because they separated from the church to set up their own. The Puritans who settled Massachusetts Bay Colony got their name because before they left England they had worked to purify the Church of England from within. Calvinists, Baptists, and other Protestant sects were established and attracted followers to their churches.

The followers of George Fox, in some ways, had the most radical ideas about religion at the time. Fox preached that Christ was within each person and that an individual did not need an organized clergy to find his or her inner religious light. He did not plan to start a new religious group, but his ideas quickly caught on. His followers soon started meeting together and formed what is known as the Society of Friends. Their meetings had no ministers, sermons, prayers, or hymns. Instead, people would sit together quietly and think about their individual relationship with God. In England and many of the colonies, the members of the Society of Friends were persecuted by the authorities. They were jailed, whipped, and even executed for their beliefs.

At one point, George Fox was in court defending his beliefs and he told the judge that he should "tremble at the word of the Lord." The judge was not impressed with Fox's warning and referred to Fox and his followers as "quakers." The name stuck. In Rhode Island, the Quakers were left to worship as they pleased and even gained a number of followers, including William Coddington.

George Fox founded the Society of Friends, or Quakers. *(Library of Congress, Prints and Photographs Division [LC-USZ62-5790])*

Most of the people who came to Rhode Island were Protestants. However, Rhode Island accepted people with other beliefs as well. In 1658, 15 Jewish families arrived in Newport from Europe. They were soon followed by Jews who had lived in the Spanish and Portuguese colonies in the Caribbean. In 1763, they joined together to create Touro Synagogue. It continues today as North America's oldest synagogue.

In 1686, yet another group arrived to take advantage of Rhode Island's religious tolerance. A group of French Huguenots came to Rhode Island. The Huguenots were French Protestants who had been forced to leave their homeland because of their religious beliefs. Many of them settled in Canada, while others immigrated to the English colonies in North America. Those who came to Rhode Island settled near the present-day town of East Greenwich.

THE NEW CHARTER

When Oliver Cromwell died in 1658, the Puritans in England found it difficult to keep control of the country. Within two years of Cromwell's death, the supporters of the monarchy had returned Charles I's son, Charles II, to the throne. During the years of the Puritan government in England, people in Massachusetts continued to interfere in Rhode Island. With the blessing of the government in Boston, the Atherton Company acquired old claims to land in parts of Rhode Island. The other colonies had a low opinion of Rhode Island, calling it "Rogue Island," "the Island of Error," and even less flattering names.

In addition to the Atherton Company, the colonies around Rhode Island claimed different parts of its territory. Connecticut claimed everything west of the Narragansett River, Plymouth claimed land on the eastern side of the bay, and Massachusetts had designs on land north of Providence. Coupled with the political uncertainties in London with the

Oliver Cromwell was a Puritan and military leader who eventually became Lord Protector of England. *(Library of Congress, Prints and Photographs Division [LC-USZ62-95711])*

Charles II ruled England, Scotland, and Ireland from 1660 until his death in 1685. *(Library of Congress, Prints and Photographs Division [LC-USZ62-96910])*

new king, many people in Rhode Island were worried. John Clarke, who had remained in London to serve as the colony's representative, went to work to try and secure Rhode Island's future.

He was finally successful when, in July 1663, Charles II issued a new charter for the colony. It was the most liberal charter received by any English colony and ensured the religious and political freedom of the colony. The document so accurately fulfilled the wishes of the people of the colony that it remained the law of the land until it was replaced by a state constitution in 1843.

Under this new charter, Rhode Island had a governor, a deputy governor, and 10 assistants. It also set up a colonial assembly with six representatives from Newport and four each from Providence, Warwick, and Portsmouth. In addition, the charter allowed for new communities that were

Excerpt from the Charter of Rhode Island and Providence Plantations
(July 15, 1663)

. . . our royall will and pleasure is, that noe person within the sayd colonye, at any tyme hereafter, shall bee any wise molested, punished, disquieted, or called in question, for any differences in opinione in matters of religion, and doe not actually disturb the civill peace of our sayd colony; but that all and everye person and persons may, from tyme to tyme, and at all tymes hereafter, freelye and fullye have and enjoye his and theire owne judgments and con-

sciences, in matters of religious concernments, throughout the tract of lance hereafter mentioned; they behaving themselves peaceablie and quietlie, and not useing this libertie to lycentiousnesse and profanenesse, nor to the civill injurye or outward disturbeance of others; any lawe, statute, or clause, therein contayned, or to bee contayned, usage or custome of this realme, to the contrary hereof, in any wise, notwithstanding.

established later to add two representatives each to the assembly. The freemen, those men who owned property, were given the right to vote in colonial elections. The only restriction required that the voters must be male Protestants. This restriction excluded the Jews and Catholics in Rhode Island from voting until after the American Revolution.

KING PHILIP'S WAR

When the Pilgrims arrived in New England and chose the site for Plymouth Colony, their nearest Indian neighbors were the Wampanoag. Their leader Massasoit helped the Pilgrims survive, and he participated in the first Thanksgiving. During his life, Massasoit maintained peace between his people and the colonists. When he died sometime in 1660, his first son, Wamsutta, became the sachem of the Wampanoag.

The leaders of Plymouth were concerned about the intentions of the new Wampanoag leader and wanted to talk to him. Wamsutta had sold more Wampanoag land to Rhode Island. The leaders of Plymouth wanted the land for their colony. They told Wamsutta, whom they called Alexander, to come to Plymouth and discuss relations between the colony and the Wampanoag. Wamsutta was ill at the time and did not answer Plymouth's summons. Rather than wait for Wamsutta to get well, the colonists sent soldiers to bring him before the leaders of Plymouth. Wamsutta's illness worsened while he was in Plymouth, and he died on his way back to his village.

His brother, Metacom (also spelled "Metacomet") whom the colonists called King Philip, became the new sachem. He blamed the colonists for contributing to his brother's death. Metacom was not willing to continue his father's good relations with the

Metacom, or King Philip, became chief of the Wampanoag in 1662. *(Library of Congress, Prints and Photographs Division [LC-USZ62-96234])*

colonists. After more than a decade of problems between colonists in Plymouth, Massachusetts, and Connecticut, Metacom united many of the Indians of New England. He almost succeeded in driving all the colonists into the Atlantic Ocean.

In January 1675, the rumors of a Native American uprising became believable for the colonists when a "Praying Indian" (an

Originally published in *Harper's New Monthly Magazine* in 1857 and quite partial to the colonists involved in the incident, this engraving illustrates the colonists' defeat of a Narragansett village in the Great Swamp of Rhode Island in December 1675. *(Library of Congress, Prints and Photographs Division [LC-USZ62-97115])*

Indian who had converted to Christianity) named John Sassamon reported to the governor of Plymouth Colony, Josiah Winslow, that Metacom was preparing for war. After telling Governor Winslow, John Sassamon was murdered. Metacom denied having any part in the murder. However, three Native Americans were captured, charged with the crime, and executed. Throughout the remainder of winter 1675, Wampanoag, Pocumtuc, and Nipmuc warriors attacked small settlements throughout the colonies. The outlying settlements, especially those in western Massachusetts in the Connecticut River Valley, felt the brunt of the early stages of the war.

In the meantime, the colonies had forced the Narragansett to sign a treaty in which they agreed to turn over all Wampanoag who might seek refuge with the Narragansett. In December 1675, Governor Josiah Winslow led a large force into Narragansett territory to make sure they were not harboring any Wampanoag. Without further negotiation or proof that the Narragansett had violated the treaty, Winslow's forces began burning Narragansett villages. On December 19, 1675, Winslow reached the Narragansetts' main village, which sat on high ground in the middle of the Great Swamp, near the current town of West Kingston, Rhode Island.

Normally, this village was a well-defended spot with water all around it. However, the winter of 1675–76 had already been a cold one, and the colonists' forces were able to reach the village by traveling over the frozen swamp. It has been estimated that 500 Narragansett warriors and an equal number of women and children were killed on that day. There was no evidence then or now that the Narragansett were ever allied with Metacom. The guerrilla warfare of the Native Americans was met with large forces of colonists and their "Praying Indian" allies killing any Native Americans they could find.

Although Rhode Island was not officially involved in King Philip's War, many people from the colony fought with the forces from Massachusetts and Connecticut. In retaliation for the Great Swamp massacre, some of the settlements in Rhode Island were attacked. When a large force of Indians came to attack Providence, Roger Williams walked out to meet them. He hoped to negotiate with Canonchet, the son of the Narragansett leader Miantonomi. Canonchet refused to reconsider, but he and his warriors walked past Williams without harming him. They then went into Providence and burned a number of houses in the town.

It soon became obvious that King Philip's War was going to end any Native Americans' hope of maintaining power in New England. Metacom was betrayed, and the colonists with their Native American allies trapped him in a swamp near New Hope, Rhode Island. When Metacom's body was finally found among the fallen, the colonial commander, Captain Benjamin Church, ordered that Metacom be decapitated and the remainder of his body cut in

Originally published in *Harper's New Monthly Magazine* in 1857 and quite partial to the colonists involved in the incident, this illustration depicts Native Americans attacking colonists in Tiverton, Rhode Island, during King Philip's War. The war's early phase included many attacks on similar small settlements. *(Library of Congress, Prints and Photographs Division [LC-USZ62-97114])*

quarters. The head was returned to Plymouth, where it was put on public display.

In the end, more than 5,000 Native Americans and more than 2,500 colonists died during King Philip's War. Many captured Native Americans were transported to the Caribbean and sold as slaves. It has been estimated that these numbers represented 40 percent of the

Dominion of New England, 1686–1689

NEW FRANCE

St. Lawrence R.

Lake Ontario

Maine
(part of Mass.)

Connecticut R.

Hudson R.

Boston

Massachusetts Bay

Massachusetts

New York

Connecticut

Plymouth

Rhode Island

Pennsylvania

Delaware R.

New York

East Jersey

Philadelphia

West Jersey

Maryland

Delaware

Virginia

ATLANTIC OCEAN

N

Dominion of New England

Other British colonies

0   100 miles
0   100 km

When James II became king of England he combined a number of colonies, including Rhode Island, into one large colony known as the Dominion of New England.

Native Americans and 5 percent of the whites in New England at the time. If that is the case, then King Philip's War was the bloodiest ever fought by North Americans.

DOMINION OF NEW ENGLAND, 1686–1689

In 1685, King Charles II died without any children to succeed him. His brother became James II, king of England. Many people in England were opposed to James II because he was a Catholic. He also turned out to be a leader who brutally punished anyone who questioned his authority. In the colonies, he was the proprietor of New York after it was captured from the Dutch. In New York, he showed that he was not interested in spreading the growing ideas of self-government.

As king, he took his ideas of autocratic rule even further in the colonies. In 1686, he combined the colonies of New England, New York, and East and West New Jersey

James II, shown in this early 19th-century engraving, ruled England for only four years. During that time, he combined Massachusetts, Maine, Plymouth, and Rhode Island to create the Dominion of New England. *(Library of Congress, Prints and Photographs Division [LC-USZ62-92123])*

into one large colony known as the Dominion of New England. At the time, there was growing hostility along the borders between the English colonies and the French in Canada. James and his advisers saw this as a way to put the colonies under the direct control of the Crown in the name of defending the colonies against the French and their Indian allies.

James named Edmund Andros governor of the Dominion of New England, and he had near-dictatorial powers. Andros only had to answer to to king. Andros suspended the colonial governments and set up his own courts. Town meetings were still allowed, but only once a year. Andros also levied taxes on the colonies without the consent of the colonists.

When it was learned that James II had been overthrown in 1688 in a bloodless rebellion referred to as the "Glorious Revolution," the

Edmund Andros ruled the Dominion of New England as its royal governor. *(Published by George Burner, 1903)*

colonists decided this was their opportunity to oust Andros. Andros had been on a military expedition in spring 1689 to the frontier to defend the dominion against raids by Native Americans allied with the French in Canada. When he got back to Boston, the local population was in rebellion. A group had been formed that called itself the "Committee for the Safety of the People." On April 18, 1689, Sir Edmund Andros was arrested and put in Boston's jail by members of the committee. Elsewhere in the dominion, Andros's appointed leaders were also removed from office. Shortly thereafter, Andros and his staff were sent back to England and the Dominion of New England ended.

James II's daughter Mary and her Dutch husband, William of Orange, became the queen and king of England in 1688. In reorganizing the colonies in New England, William and Mary combined Plymouth and Massachusetts into the royal colony of Massachusetts with a new charter. They also reaffirmed the 1664 charter of Rhode Island. William and Mary soon found themselves involved in a war in Europe known as the War of the League of Augsburg. When the war spilled over to North America, it was simply called King William's War as fighting worsened between the French and English colonies. Rhode Island was protected from the fighting by its location. However, ships from Rhode Island took part in the war. Privately owned ships that had a commission from the Crown to attack enemy shipping were called privateers.

Life in Rhode Island

The first settlers to arrive in Rhode Island survived much as their Indian neighbors did. They raised corn and other crops suited to the area, hunted in the forests, and fished in the rivers

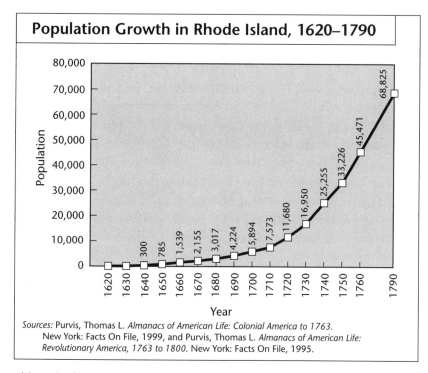

Population Growth in Rhode Island, 1620–1790

Sources: Purvis, Thomas L. *Almanacs of American Life: Colonial America to 1763.* New York: Facts On File, 1999, and Purvis, Thomas L. *Almanacs of American Life: Revolutionary America, 1763 to 1800.* New York: Facts On File, 1995.

Although Rhode Island's population was small in comparison to colonies such as Massachusetts and Virginia, Rhode Islanders prospered as farmers and merchants.

and bays. As time went on, they planted European crops such as oats and peas that grew well in Rhode Island's mild climate. They also planted orchards. William Blackstone, the first European to settle in Rhode Island, was well known for developing new varieties of apples that thrived. The colonists also raised domestic farm animals, cleared more pastures, and cut the abundant marsh grasses that grew along the edges of the bay to use as hay in the winter.

By 1700, there were almost 6,000 non-Indian people in Rhode Island, and a number of new towns had grown up around the bay. Although this may not seem like very many people (the two largest colonies, Massachusetts and Virginia, had between 55,000 and 60,000 settlers each), Rhode Island prospered. The colonists were soon growing a surplus of food, and a number of big farms had large flocks of sheep and were exporting wool. This surplus of agricultural products and the number of good harbors in Narragansett Bay turned many toward the sea to make their living.

TRADERS FROM RHODE ISLAND

At first, Rhode Island's surplus products were traded in New York and Boston, where there were large numbers of people. However, the traders were soon going farther and farther from home, developing new trade routes and participating in existing trade. One of the first places outside of North America that Rhode Island traders went was to the Caribbean. There they were able to sell food, wood, and other essentials to the large colonial sugar plantations that were worked by slaves.

Rather than sail back to New England with their ships empty, the traders brought back sugar and molasses. Much of the molasses was turned into rum, which became one of the major exports of New England, and much of it was carried in Rhode Island ships. Rum and other New England products were soon being traded in locations around the Atlantic Ocean. As time went on, Rhode Island ship owners decided there was another cargo that they could carry that would make them very wealthy. In the 18th century, Rhode Island merchants became deeply involved in the trade in African slaves.

SLAVE TRADERS

Tribes living along the west coast of the African continent had long been in the business of raiding neighboring tribes and selling their captives as slaves. At first, a number of European countries enslaved the Native Americans of the Caribbean, Central, and South American. When those people died off, primarily from European diseases, African slaves were brought to the colonies in the Americas. The Spanish, Portuguese, and especially the Dutch were involved in the slave trade. Slavery was accepted and practiced in all the English colonies in the Caribbean as well.

At first, the English colonies in North America tried to use indentured servants as a cheap source of labor. Although many people came to the colonies as indentured servants, this did not work out well on the plantations in the Southern colonies. As time went by, slaves became the primary source of labor on the plantations in the South and made up a substantial portion of the population. By 1750, 31 percent of the population in Maryland was of African descent, and most of them were slaves. In Virginia, African

Indentured Servants

The cost of getting to North America was often more than many of the people who wanted to come could afford. Almost as soon as people started coming to the American colonies, they brought workers with them who were under contract to them. They paid for their passage in exchange for a number of years of labor. These contracts were called indentures. The people who worked under them were called indentured servants. Indentures varied in length from three to seven years, and people were often promised cash bonuses for completion of their indentures.

People agreed to become indentured servants because they believed that life would be better for them in the colonies than in England even if they had to be other people's servants for a period of time. Many indentured servants served as agricultural workers, especially in the Chesapeake Bay area. Many died because of the harsh working conditions on plantations. In colonies such as Rhode Island, indentured servants worked in a wide variety of occupations. Some served as household servants or worked as laborers on the larger farms. Many also worked as apprentices in a wide variety of trades.

Narragansett Pacer

Horses were an important part of life in Rhode Island and valuable as a trade commodity. The horse breeders of Rhode Island created one of the most popular breeds of the 18th century. It was known as the Narragansett pacer and was sought after throughout the colonies of the Caribbean and North America. The Narragansett pacer was reported to have a fast, smooth pacing gait that allowed it to cover a mile in little more than two minutes. George Washington was reported to own one, and Paul Revere supposedly borrowed one for his famous ride from Cambridge to Lexington to warn the minutemen. Narragansett pacers played a role in the development of a number of breeds, including the standardbred, saddlebred, and the Tennessee walking horse. At the beginning of the 19th century, the roads in the Northeast had improved to the point where people preferred to travel by coach and carriage rather than ride, and the Narragansett pacer disappeared.

Americans made up 44 percent of the population. In South Carolina, the population was 61 percent African American.

While the vast majority of slaves in the South worked in the fields, the few slaves in the North were more likely to be servants in the homes of wealthy white people. In states such as Massachusetts and Pennsylvania, the population in 1750 was only about 2 percent African-American. The northern state with the largest percentage of people of African descent was Rhode Island. There African Americans made up 10 percent of the population. The slaves in Rhode Island worked as servants and on the large estates of the wealthy.

On Rhode Island's large farms, sheep and cattle raising were the main activities. The owners of the slaves and the farms lived more in the style of southern plantation owners than that of the traditionally thrifty New England farmers. They had the leisure time to act like the nobility in England, spending time fox hunting and holding horse races.

The slave traders of Rhode Island transported 20 percent of the slaves imported into the Americas, including many of the slaves who ended up on the sugar plantations of the Caribbean. Slave markets were active in Newport, Bristol, and Providence. The trade in African slaves created what is called the triangular trade for the merchants of Rhode Island.

THE TRIANGULAR TRADE

The triangular trade for the merchants of Rhode Island involved taking rum and other goods produced in New England to Africa, where they were traded for slaves. Most slaves were then brought to the Caribbean. Many slave owners in the South preferred to buy slaves who had already been working in the Caribbean because those people were thought to be more accepting of their fate than

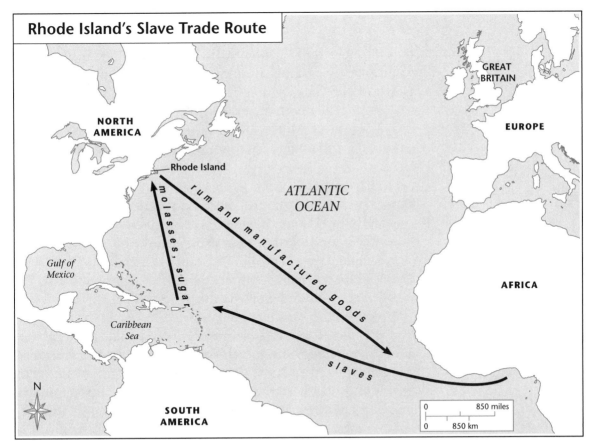

Of all the American colonies, Rhode Island was the most active in the slave trade. Rhode Island ships sailed from Rhode Island with rum and other manufactured goods to Africa, where they traded for slaves. Most slaves were taken to the Caribbean, where they were traded for sugar and molasses. The sugar and molasses was then brought back to Rhode Island, where it was distilled into rum.

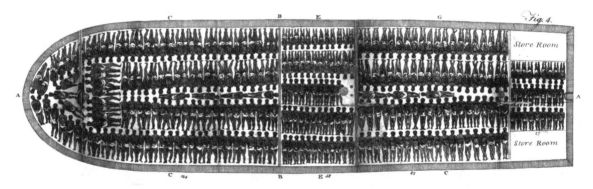

In this detail from a 1780s etching, captured Africans are crammed into the hold of a British slave ship, the *Brookes,* similar in design to many others used to transport slaves. *(Library of Congress, Prints and Photographs Division [LC-USZ62-44000])*

slaves brought directly from Africa. In the Caribbean, the ships would take on a load of sugar and molasses destined for the distilleries of New England to be made into rum.

The most infamous leg of the triangle was the so-called middle passage from Africa to the Americas. The passage took between 25 and 60 days, depending on wind conditions. During that time, the slaves were poorly treated, getting a small allotment of food twice a day. The slaves were brought up on deck during the day, but the men were kept in shackles. The women and children were often allowed to move about freely. At night or if the weather was bad, the slaves were forced to remain below deck, where they were allowed only as much space as was needed to lie down.

During the middle passage, many slaves died. The death toll depended on the weather: The longer the trip and/or the more the slaves were confined below deck, the more that died. Spoiled food or contaminated water also killed many on the slave ships. The development of faster ships in the second half of the 18th century and a better understanding of diseases such as dysentery and scurvy reduced the number of deaths in the middle passage.

It is estimated that more than 10 million Africans traveled the middle passage into slavery in the Americas. Many of those who came died within a few years. In the first official census of the United States in 1790, there were almost 700,000 slaves in a total population of some 3.9 million people.

PIRATES AND PRIVATEERS

Between 1689 and 1762, four wars were fought between France and Great Britain. The portions of these wars that were fought in North America are collectively known as the French and Indian wars. They are called that because many of the Native Americans in Canada and along the frontier of the English colonies fought on the side of the French. Although there was only one attack on Rhode Island territory during this time, Rhode Island supplied troops and transport for a number of campaigns. Rhode Islanders took part in the attack on Cartagena, Colombia, in 1741, in which almost the entire English force died either in battle or of disease. In 1745, when a combined colonial and British force captured the French fort at Louisbourg on Cape Breton Island, which is now part of Nova Scotia, Rhode Island sailors and ship captains provided transportation for the colonial forces. Rhode Islanders were also a part of the final campaign against the French strongholds of Quebec and Montreal at the end of the fourth and final war in 1762.

Although Rhode Island soldiers fought alongside soldiers from the other colonies, the major contribution from Narragansett Bay in these wars was the numerous privateers who sailed out to attack enemy shipping. *Privateer* is the term used to describe the people involved and the ships they sailed on. The

The Attack on Block Island
(May 1689)

During King William's War, which was the first of the French and Indian wars, seven French privateers attacked Block Island, off the coast of Rhode Island, in May 1689. After easily capturing the island, the French locked many of the island's residents into one of the houses, then proceeded to ransack the island. They took everything of value. When word reached Newport of the capture of Block Island, two ships with 90 soldiers were sent to rescue the island. At first it looked like the French would hold off the Americans, but after a two-hour battle, the French sailed away. The French commander was caught off the coast of Connecticut and was killed.

Under the command of William Pepperell, a volunteer militia with members from Massachusetts, Connecticut, and New Hampshire defeated the French in Canada at Louisbourg, Cape Breton Island. Sailors and ship captains from Rhode Island provided transportation. *(Library of Congress, Prints and Photographs Division [LC-USZ62-105732])*

ships were privately owned, and the ship owners were given permission either by the colony or the Crown to attack enemy merchant ships. At the time, navies were not big enough to patrol all the waters of Europe's far-reaching empires, so it was a common practice for governments to employ private ships during wars.

A privateer was allowed to attack any ship flying the flag of an enemy country. Privateers and the owners of their ships were paid only if they were successful in capturing the ships of the enemy and the goods they carried. When a privateer captured a ship, it was brought into port, where the ship and its cargo would be sold. The profits would be split among the owner of the privateer and its crew, with people getting shares based on their rank. It is estimated that during King George's War (1744–48) alone, more than 100 French ships were captured by Rhode Island privateers. Many privateers became rich during these wars. Some even found that attacking fairly defenseless merchant ships was such an easy way to make a living that they continued to do so even when there were no wars. Others went to the extreme of attacking the ships of Britain's allies during the wars. In these two ways, some privateers crossed the line and became pirates.

Pirates such as Captain William Kidd often sold their stolen goods to colonists for a much lower price than the colonists could purchase legitimate goods. In this early 20th-century painting, Captain Kidd welcomes a young woman aboard his ship so she may look at his goods. *(Library of Congress, Prints and Photographs Division [LC-USZC2-6373])*

Piracy was a common problem in the 17th and 18th centuries. For a time, pirates were welcome in the harbors of Rhode Island. It has been reported that Samuel Cranston, who was governor of the colony from 1698 to 1727, was friendly to many pirates. As Rhode Island was struggling to compete with its large neighbor colonies, pirates provided a source of profit for many around Narragansett Bay. First, the stolen goods they brought into port were sold much more cheaply than the same goods that arrived in the colony by legal means. The pirates also had gold and silver money to spend. Money was always scarce in the colonies, and cash-paying customers in Rhode Island were not asked where the money came from.

Piracy in Rhode Island and other colonies became so widespread that the Crown tried to put a stop to it. At first, the attempts were ignored by the people of Rhode Island. However, as legitimate trade grew in the colony, Governor Cranston was forced to act. On July 19, 1723, 26 pirates were hanged in Newport, and Narragansett Bay was no longer a haven for pirates. From that point on, the merchants and people of Rhode Island were more likely to conduct business according to the laws of the colony and the Crown. After the French and Indian wars, attempts to raise money for the Crown by taxing and regulating

William Kidd
(ca. 1645–1701)

One of the most famous pirates to sail into Narragansett Bay was Captain William Kidd. Captain Kidd was born in Scotland and had gone to sea early in his life. He ended up in New York and soon was captain of his own ship. In 1695, he was asked to become a privateer for the Crown. He sailed to Madagascar, off the east coast of Africa, where he was supposed to put an end to pirates in the area that were attacking English shipping. Instead, he turned to piracy and captured a number of ships in 1697 and 1698. When he returned to the Americas in 1699, he learned that a warrant had been issued for his capture. He immediately sailed to New York and then Boston to try and clear his name. Instead, he was sent to London where he was tried and hanged on May 23, 1701.

After leaving New York, he had buried some of his treasure on Gardiner's Island, at the eastern end of Long Island. Between New York and Boston, it is reported that he stopped in Rhode Island, where he visited with merchants who supposedly were his partners. Many believed that Captain Kidd hid more treasure on Block Island and Conanicut Island in Narragansett Bay. The Gardiner's Island treasure was found shortly after it was buried. The treasure in Rhode Island, if it exists, has never been found.

Captain Kidd was hanged in London on May 23, 1701. This illustration of his death appeared in an early 20th-century book about pirates. *(Library of Congress, Prints and Photographs Division [LC-USZ62-95356])*

trade in the colonies turned many Rhode Island traders to smuggling and other activities to protest the interference of the Crown in the colonies.

Road to Revolution

By the end of the French and Indian wars in 1762, much had changed in the thirteen colonies in North America. No longer were they the struggling outposts that had existed 100 years before. By this time, there were more than 1.5 million people in the colonies, and many of them considered themselves Americans first and British subjects second, if at all. Most colonists were now native born. Many of them were descendants of Scots, Irish, Germans, and other Europeans who had come to the colonies looking for a better life than they could hope for in Europe.

At this time, Britain was changing. The country was becoming more industrialized and needed its colonies for two reasons. First, the British needed raw materials for their industries and, second and even more important, they needed markets for their goods. Over time, many laws were passed to regulate trade within the British Empire to favor the ship owners, merchants, and factory owners in Britain. For the most part, these laws, known collectively as the Navigation Acts, were ignored in the North American colonies, especially as they applied to the trade in molasses.

There were at least 30 distilleries in Rhode Island making rum primarily as a commodity to be traded for slaves in Africa. To make the maximum profit, molasses had to be bought at the lowest possible price. The lowest prices could be found in the non-English colonies in the Caribbean. To get around the duties (taxes) imposed by the Navigation Acts, it was common practice to

Many British colonies in the Caribbean produced sugar from sugarcane. In this mid-18th-century British engraving, an overseer directs some Native peoples (possibly in the West Indies) while they process sugarcane. *(Library of Congress, Prints and Photographs Division [LC-USZ62-7841])*

smuggle molasses into the colony and bribe customs officials to turn a blind eye on the trade in foreign molasses. Some traders even continued to import molasses from French Caribbean colonies when France and Britain were at war. To win the French and Indian wars, the government in London had gone deeply in debt, and it was now faced with the need to defend a much larger piece of North America. Starting with the Sugar Act of 1764, Parliament enacted a number of laws that were intended to pay for at least the cost of administering the English colonies in North America. However, these laws had the completely opposite effect, as they led to the Declaration of Independence and the American Revolution.

THE SUGAR ACT OF 1764

An earlier Navigation Act, known as the Molasses Act of 1733, had proven ineffective in helping English sugar growers and did not raise any revenue for the Crown's customs offices. One of the reasons people had smuggled molasses was that the tax of sixpence a gallon charged by the 1733 act made imported molasses far too expensive for the distillers to make a profit. This is why so much smuggling took place in Rhode Island and Massachusetts, which had a large number of rum distilleries. Under the Sugar Act, the duty was cut in half. The leaders in London felt that if the tax was reduced, people would be more willing to pay it.

In addition to reducing the tax, the law made a number of changes in the way violators were prosecuted and in the way customs authorities went about their business. In the past, customs violations were tried in local courts where the friends, neighbors, and employees of the smugglers served on the juries. The few cases that were brought before these local courts were almost never decided in favor of the Crown. In Rhode Island and Massachusetts, the reaction to the Sugar Act was loudest. In Massachusetts, it took the form of letters from local merchants to the king and Parliament protesting the Sugar Act. In Rhode Island, the arrival of British naval vessels in Narragansett Bay to enforce the new and existing trade laws caused serious and sometimes violent reactions.

When the British naval vessels *Squirrel* and *St. John* began patrolling the waters around Newport, they quickly found themselves testing the willingness of Rhode Island to give in to the Crown's authority over trade. When the ship *Basto* illegally tried to land a cargo of molasses on the east side of Aquidneck Island, the ship and its cargo were seized by the *St. John*. Lieutenant Thomas Hill, commanding officer of the *St. John*, must have been amazed when he brought the *Basto* into Newport Harbor.

Instead of being thanked by grateful customs officials, he was told he had no authority to take the ship. He immediately headed for Boston to seek clarification from higher authorities. While he was gone, it is reported, one of his crewmen deserted. When his officers and other crew members went ashore to capture the deserter, they were met by an angry mob and were forced to retreat to their ship. When it looked like the mob was coming after the *St. John* by boat, the *St. John* headed out to sea. The colonists took over the cannons in the fort and fired at least eight shots at the departing *St. John*. They might have done more than shoot a hole in the ship's mainsail had not the *Squirrel* put itself between the fort and the *St. John* and brought its 22 cannons to bear on the colonists.

Because of this incident and other protests, the tax on molasses was reduced even further, to onepence a gallon. This served to quiet some of the discontent in the colonies, but it meant that the Sugar Act would do little to raise the money needed by Parliament to alleviate the high taxes that were being paid by residents of England. Parliament's next attempt to raise money in the colonies created an even greater reaction.

THE STAMP ACT, March 22, 1765

The Stamp Act of 1765 was intended to have the same result as the earlier Sugar Act, and that was to pay for some of the cost of keeping a military force in the Americas. The stamp tax, which required that an official stamp be purchased and applied to a variety of goods, was not a new concept. It was a common practice in England and had even been used by some of the American colonies. The same principle is still used in the United States today as state and federal taxes are applied to products like cigarettes and alcohol, although actual stamps are no longer used. In this instance, stamps were to be placed on all legal documents, newspapers, and other printed materials, as well as some consumer items such as playing cards.

When affixed to goods, this stamp signified that a tax must be paid upon purchase. Many colonists felt that the British unfairly introduced these taxes when they implemented the Stamp Act in 1765, which affected goods and services ranging from business transactions to playing cards. *(Library of Congress, Prints and Photographs Division [LC-USZ61-539])*

The problem for the Americans was not the idea of paying taxes, although nobody likes paying taxes. They were concerned that they

Sons of Liberty

When the Stamp Act was passed by Parliament in 1765, people in the colonies formed groups in their communities to protest the act. One of the few opponents of the Stamp Act in Parliament's House of Commons, Isaac Barré, called the protestors the "sons of liberty." Soon the name spread to the colonies, where it was readily adopted. Various Sons of Liberty groups organized protests in Rhode Island and would later hold "tea parties" in Boston, New Jersey, and South Carolina when the Tea Act was passed.

Colonists denounce the Stamp Act in 1765. *(Library of Congress)*

had no representation in Parliament. It was thought that a legislative body could tax only the people who had elected it. The cry in the colonies became "No taxation without representation." There was little opposition to the Stamp Act in Parliament, while the reaction against the act in the colonies was widespread and often resulted in mob action led by groups calling themselves the Sons of Liberty.

One of the first protests in Rhode Island was again aimed at a British naval vessel in Narragansett Bay. On June 4, 1765, a mob of about 500 protesters seized one of the small ship's boats from the warship *Maidstone*, which was anchored in Newport Harbor. Some of the crew of the *Maidstone* were ashore, trying to impress local residents into the navy. This was a legal practice in England where people were forced into the navy. The Newport mob carried the boat to the town common and burned it.

In addition to the burning of the *Maidstone*'s boat, the people of Rhode Island participated in protests that were similar to those in

The Rights of Colonies Examined
1764

In the years leading up to the American Revolution, a number of Patriots wrote about the struggle between Parliament and the colonies, and these writings were published in pamphlets. One of the most famous of these pamphlets was *Common Sense,* written by Thomas Paine in 1776. Before that, in 1764, Governor Stephen Hopkins of Rhode Island wrote an essay entitled *The Rights of Colonies Examined.* It was published as a pamphlet and outlined the relationship between the colonies and the government in London. Hopkins made it clear that the Crown had done very little to support the colonies in the previous 150 years and therefore should not expect much in return as it tried to raise funds by taxing the colonies.

Stephen Hopkins governed Rhode Island from 1756 to 1764 and was very active in the Revolutionary War. Located on Hopkins Street in Providence, Rhode Island, this house, shown in a 1958 photograph, belonged to Hopkins and is now a museum. *(Library of Congress, Prints and Photographs Division [HABS, RI,4-PROV,32-8])*

Much of Rhode Island's coastline is contained in Narragansett Bay. This 1765 drawing shows a small ship anchored in Bristol, Rhode Island, which borders the bay. *(Library of Congress, Prints and Photographs Division [LC-USZ62-45382])*

other colonies. On August 26, 1765, the man who was appointed to be the stamp agent in Newport, Augustus Johnston, and two Tory (those loyal to the Crown) leaders, Dr. Thomas Moffat and Martin Howard, Jr., were startled to find dummies representing them hanging on a gallows in the center of town. The three men were forced to seek safety on a British navy ship in the harbor while the mob turned violent and destroyed the homes of Moffat and Howard. Johnston was forced to publicly resign as stamp

agent, while Moffat and Howard went to London to see if they could get the Crown to revoke Rhode Island's charter and make it a royal colony.

The colonies, which usually went their own way, were so upset by the Stamp Act that they convened a meeting in New York City in October 1765. Nine colonies, including Rhode Island, sent two delegates, Henry Ward and Metcalf Bower, to what is known as the Stamp Act Congress. As a result of the congress, a letter was sent to King George III asking him to intervene with Parliament on behalf of the colonies. Although there was little talk of independence or revolution at this time, the reaction to the Stamp Act was so strong and far-reaching in the colonies that only Georgia ever issued any stamps. The other colonies either ignored the stamps or found clever ways to avoid them. In Newport, more than 80 ships left port in the week before the act was supposed to go into effect on November 1, 1765, to avoid getting their papers stamped. Usually around 10 ships would have sailed during the same period of time. On November 1, 1765, a mock funeral was held for "liberty" in Newport. In 1766, the Stamp Act was repealed and many colonists celebrated their victory.

In an effort to show that they were not giving in completely to the colonists, when Parliament repealed the Stamp Act, the members passed the Declaratory Act. This stated that although they were repealing the Stamp Act, they wanted the colonies to know that Parliament had the right to make any laws they saw fit to govern

George III ruled Great Britain and Ireland from 1760 until 1820. *(Library of Congress)*

and tax the colonies. Had Parliament left it there, the 13 colonies might still be part of the British Commonwealth, but additional attempts to tax and regulate the colonies led to war.

THE TOWNSHEND DUTIES,
June 29, 1767

When the Stamp Act failed, Parliament tried again. One complaint about the Stamp Act had been that it was a direct tax on the people of the colonies. This time, under the leadership of Charles Townshend, in 1767, Parliament passed the Townshend Duties on specific goods that were regularly imported into the colonies. These included paper, glass, lead, painter's colors, and tea. A duty is an indirect tax that is paid by the merchant, and therefore, no one in Parliament expected the colonists to object. Although the reaction was not as strong or as universal as that against the Stamp Act, many colonists began a boycott of English goods.

It took a while for the boycott to gain momentum. Merchants were especially reluctant to join in, as they would suffer the most if they had no goods to sell. The merchants in Rhode Island were especially unwilling to participate. They had less in the way of locally produced goods and were more dependent on trade with England and the rest of Europe for their business. Eventually, the merchants of Rhode Island gave in and joined the boycott when other colonies threatened to include Rhode Island shippers in their boycott.

During this time, the British naval patrols in Narragansett Bay and along the Connecticut coast continued to upset the people of Rhode Island. In July 1769, the British sloop *Liberty* sailed into Newport, followed by two trading ships from Connecticut that were charged with smuggling. A mob led by the Sons of Liberty once again took action. They forced the crew of the *Liberty* to go ashore and then towed the sloop out to Goat Island. They emptied the contents of the *Liberty* into the harbor and then burned the sloop in shallow water.

By this time, British soldiers were stationed in the major cities of the colonies. On January 18, 1770, soldiers and colonists clashed in what is known as the Battle of Golden Hill, in New York. No one was killed, but many were injured. The same cannot be said of the confrontation that took place in Boston on March 5, 1770. At that time, a large group confronted soldiers in front of the Boston Customs House. The mob taunted the soldiers and threw ice and snow at them. Although no one apparently gave the order, the soldiers opened fire on the crowd, killing five in what has become known as the Boston Massacre.

In Rhode Island, the major conflict continued to be between the needs of people to use Narragansett Bay as their primary way to transport themselves and goods around Rhode Island and the attempt by the British navy to control the bay. British lieutenant

William Dudingston had become infamous around the bay as he commanded the ship *Gaspee*. Dudingston reportedly harassed all manner of boats and ships and even seized legal cargoes. He also

The Browns of Providence

Four brothers—Nicholas, Joseph, Moses, and John Brown—were the leading merchants in Providence at this time. As their wealth increased, they gave much back to their town. They helped have schools and churches built as well as other improvements to the town. Together they helped found Rhode Island College, the colony's first college, in 1764. Later, when Nicholas Brown's son Nicholas contributed to the college, the name was changed to Brown College and then Brown University. It is Rhode Island's oldest college and the seventh oldest in America.

In 1764 in Providence, Rhode Island, the Brown brothers founded Rhode Island College, which was later renamed Brown University. In 1770, University Hall, shown in a 1937 photograph, was built as part of the college. *(Library of Congress, Prints and Photographs Division [HABS, RI,4-PROV,81A-1])*

Published in the early 20th century, this image shows angry residents of Rhode Island burning the *Gaspee,* a British ship, in 1772. Above the scene flies a Rhode Island regimental flag, which is somewhat similar to the contemporary Rhode Island state flag. *(Library of Congress, Prints and Photographs Division [LC-USZ62-107624])*

regularly sent his crew ashore to raid farms for livestock and other produce. People in Newport complained to British authorities about the actions of the *Gaspee*, but their complaints were ignored.

On the night of June 9, 1772, the *Gaspee* was pursuing the trading sloop *Hannah*, which was headed for Providence. Captain Benjamin Lindsey of the *Hannah* was from Newport, and he knew the bay well. With the *Gaspee* close behind, he sailed directly for Namquit Point. At the last possible moment, Lindsey turned his smaller and more maneuverable *Hannah* away from the sandbar in front of the point. Dudingston realized what was happening too late, and the *Gaspee* ran up onto the sandbar.

All the British could do was wait a few hours until high tide, when they would be able to float off the sandbar. In the meantime, Lindsey sailed on to Providence, where he told the merchant John Brown what had happened and where the *Gaspee* was. Brown quickly gathered a group of men into a number of longboats and headed for the stranded *Gaspee*. They wrapped their oars in cloth so they could approach the ship silently, and they were not noticed until they were very close. When a crew member on deck challenged the boats, the Patriots continued toward the ship without responding.

When Dudingston came on deck, he reportedly challenged the Patriots in the boats. Captain Abraham Whipple, who would later be one of the first commanders in the American navy, responded that they had a warrant for his arrest. Before Whipple had finished talking, someone among the Patriots shot the hated British lieutenant. The Americans quickly boarded the ship while the British crew hid below deck. Dudingston's wound was treated, he and his crew were taken off the ship, and the *Gaspee* was set on fire. Later, the name of Namquit Point was changed to Gaspee Point to commemorate the victory of Rhode Island Patriots over the *Gaspee*.

After the burning of the *Gaspee*, a special investigation was begun to find out who was responsible. No one was ever charged, and the commission really did not seem that interested in finding the culprits. In 1770, all of the Townshend Duties were repealed except for the one on tea. The duty on tea was more a symbolic gesture on the part of Parliament than a real attempt to continue the battle with the colonies over taxes. It would take another act of Parliament to bring the situation in the colonies to the boiling point.

THE TEA ACT,
May 10, 1773

In 1773, the British East India Company was in financial trouble and many influential people in England had a stake in the company. As it stood, all the tea that the company brought from Asia had to be shipped to England. There it was sold to wholesalers who marked it up and sold it to other wholesalers around the world. By the time the tea importers in the colonies marked it up and paid the tea tax left over from the Townshend Duties, British tea was extremely expensive. Dutch tea that was smuggled into the colonies was much cheaper. To help the East India Company, Parliament passed the Tea Act of 1773. This law cut out the middlemen and gave the East India Company exclusive rights to sell tea in the American colonies.

If no one had reacted to the Tea Act, British tea would have actually been cheaper than the smuggled Dutch tea. However, many Patriots saw the monopoly that was being given to the East India Company as just one more attempt by Parliament to dictate

To protect the passage of the Tea Act, some male colonists, disguised as American Indians, boarded three ships in Boston Harbor on December 16, 1773, and dumped hundreds of cases of tea into the water. The event became known as the Boston Tea Party. *(Library of Congress)*

to the colonies. The Tea Act was also going to affect a number of merchants who had been in the tea business but had not been selected to sell tea for the East India Company. When the first shipment of tea arrived in Boston, on December 16, 1773, a group of the Sons of Liberty disguised themselves as Indians and boarded the ships that had brought the tea. Careful not to damage the ships or injure anyone, the "Indians" threw £10,000 worth of tea in the harbor.

After the Boston Tea Party, similar events were held in other colonies. New York, New Jersey, and South Carolina all had their own "Tea Parties." Throughout the colonies, people boycotted English tea. They made "liberty tea" from a number of native plants or continued to buy smuggled tea that came from the Dutch.

The Boston Tea Party was the final push that was needed to bring the two sides to the point of no return. Parliament reacted swiftly and forcefully. It was ready to put the colonies in their place. Parliament passed a series of laws known as the Coercive Acts, which were meant to force the people of Boston and the colonies in general to submit to the authority of the Crown. Wars start for a variety of reasons, and the American Revolution is no exception. Political, financial, and social issues were all involved over a number of years in bringing the two sides to war.

7

The War for Independence

THE INTOLERABLE ACTS, 1774

Starting in March 1774, Parliament passed a series of five laws that were intended to bring the thirteen colonies back under the control of the Crown. To the members of the government in London, these acts were known as the Coercive Acts. The Patriots were extremely upset by these acts and referred to them as the Intolerable Acts. The first one was called the Boston Port Act. It closed the port of Boston until the tea that had been dumped in the harbor was paid for. Throughout the colonies, people were appalled that the Crown did this. Because the port was closed, businesses in Boston were forced to close, and without ships coming into Boston Harbor, food and other needed supplies soon began to run short.

The idea that the Crown could do the same to any other port in the colonies if it was provoked was a wake-up call to many colonists. People in Rhode Island were very aware of how dependent they were on their own harbors, and many were sympathetic with the people of Boston. Rhode Islanders sent food overland to Boston to help the people there. Other colonies helped as well, and some of that food was shipped to Rhode Island ports and then taken overland to Boston.

The second act was the Massachusetts Government Act, which passed on May 20, 1774. This law changed the government in

The Wanton-Lyman-Hazard House, shown in a 20th-century photograph, is the oldest surviving house in Newport, Rhode Island. Built in the 1670s, the house has been owned (as its name demonstrates) by many people. Richard Ward, elected governor of Rhode Island in 1741 and father of Samuel Ward, who also governed Rhode Island, owned the house for some time. *(Library of Congress, Prints and Photographs Division [HABS, RI,3-NEWP,12-1])*

Massachusetts, giving the Crown much more control of the colony. In Rhode Island, where the colonists had more political and religious freedom than any other colony, the idea of the crown interfering with their colonial government was very upsetting.

The next two acts dealt with court cases and the housing of soldiers in the colonies. Passed on May 20, 1774, the Administration of Justice Act made it possible for the Crown to move court cases to other colonies or even to England. This was to remove cases from sympathetic colonial juries. The Quartering Act required a colony to pay for the British troops that were stationed within its borders. The fifth act was the Quebec Act. Although this act dealt with Canada, it angered Patriots in the thirteen colonies because it seemed to treat the people of Canada more favorably than those in the other English colonies in North America.

Throughout the colonies and especially in New England, local militia groups were organized. They began to prepare to defend their homes from British troops. To counteract the loss of local control of government, Committees of Correspondence were formed in the colonies to create a way for the Patriots to communicate with each other. Rhode Island was the first colony to

The First Continental Congress met in Philadelphia in September 1774 and composed and sent resolutions to the king of Britain. The delegates planned a second congress for the following spring to assess their situation. *(Library of Congress, Prints and Photographs Division [LC-USZ62-45328])*

suggest that the colonies get together as they had at the Stamp Act Congress. They selected Stephen Hopkins and Samuel Ward to represent the colony. Soon the people in other colonies saw that a continental congress was indeed needed, and the colonies agreed to send representatives to Philadelphia in September 1774.

THE FIRST CONTINENTAL CONGRESS, September 5, 1774, to October 26, 1774

When the delegates arrived in Philadelphia, Pennsylvania, for the First Continental Congress on September 5, 1774, they had differing instructions from their colonial governments. Rhode Island gave Hopkins and Ward the authority to call upon King George III to address the problems that faced the colonies. They also felt it was time for the colonies to hold an annual congress so they could work together to solve their problems with the Crown and Parliament.

The First Continental Congress had three primary accomplishments. The delegates sent a list of grievances to George III. They also agreed to promote a boycott of English goods. Finally, they agreed to meet again in spring 1775.

THE WAR BEGINS

Between the time the First Continental Congress adjourned and the opening of the Second Continental Congress in May 1775, the situation in the colonies took a drastic turn. Before April 1775, the large British force in Boston had been willing to stay in the city while the Patriot leaders and the local militia prepared for a fight. On April 14, 1775, General

Thomas Gage, the British commander in Boston, received orders from England directing him to use force to control the Patriot activities in the colony.

On the night of April 18, 1775, Gage sent a force of 800 soldiers out from Boston to capture the Patriot leaders John Hancock and Samuel Adams. He also instructed his troops to seize a supply of guns and ammunition the Patriots had stored in Concord. It was at this time that Paul Revere, William Dawes, and others rode out from Boston to warn the Patriots that the British were on the way.

The next morning, April 19, 1775, when the British force arrived at Lexington Common there were approximately 70

The Battles of Lexington and Concord signaled the beginning of the Revolutionary War. In this engraving, the colonists and the British fight at the Battle of Lexington. *(Library of Congress, Prints and Photographs Division [LC-USZ62-8623])*

colonial militiamen waiting for them. When the British ordered the colonials to surrender, instead they tried to escape. No one knows who fired the first shot, but it set off a volley from the British troops that killed eight and wounded 10 colonists. Adams and Hancock had already fled the area, so the British marched on to Concord, where they were met by a much larger colonial force. At the North Bridge in Concord, the British were forced to retreat toward Boston. As the British marched back to the city, the colonial militia hid in the woods along the way and picked off soldier after soldier. By the time they got back to Boston, 273 British soldiers had been killed or wounded.

When word of the Battles of Lexington and Concord spread, it was obvious to all that any hopes of a peaceful solution with the Crown had ended. In Rhode Island, Captain James Wallace, the British naval commander in Newport, threatened to burn the town if any colonials went to join the Patriot forces that were rushing to Boston. Despite Wallace's threats, many Rhode Island Patriots, led by Nathanael Greene, headed to Boston.

THE SECOND CONTINENTAL CONGRESS

When the Second Continental Congress opened on May 10, 1775, the delegates were confronted with a war. A huge force of colonial militia was gathering around Boston, hoping to drive the British out of the city. As the congress debated, the situation in Rhode Island grew violent. To supply his troops in Boston, General Gage had the navy raid Rhode Island and other nearby areas to seize food and livestock. On June 3, 1775, the local militia in Rhode Island stopped a force of 100 sailors from seizing a supply of flour. On June 15, 1775, sailors from one of the British warships took a ship that was bringing supplies to Providence from New York. A small Rhode Island sloop retook the supply ship and brought it into Newport to the cheers of the Patriots in the community.

Two days later, on June 17, 1775, the first major battle of the war was fought at Bunker Hill in Charlestown, Massachusetts, on the north shore of Boston Harbor. Although the colonial forces eventually lost the battle, they inflicted so many casualties that the British leaders were reluctant to engage in another

The Second Continental Congress convened on May 10, 1775, and remained in session until the newly independent United States had a constitution. *(National Archives, Still Picture Records, NWDNS-148-CCD-35)*

The Continental Navy

As Esek Hopkins tried to piece together a navy to go up against the largest and most powerful navy in the world, he turned to Rhode Island for ships and sailors. Hopkins had sailed the world as a merchant and as a privateer and soon had a force of eight ships ranging in size from 8 guns to 36 guns, manned mostly by Rhode Islanders. His first mission was to attack the Bahamas, where he easily captured Nassau. In Nassau, Hopkins's tiny navy seized cannons, powder, and shot cannon balls to help supply the struggling Continental forces.

On their way back to the colonies on April 6, 1776, Hopkins and his fleet encountered Captain Wallace's British ships off Block Island. In a battle that lasted 24 hours, the Americans were able to escape after suffering serious damage to a number of their ships. The damage done to the fledgling navy almost put an end to it. From that point forward, the Americans depended much more on privateers than on its own navy to help the cause. Many of the privateers were from Rhode Island.

pitched battle with the colonial forces surrounding Boston. At about the same time, the Continental Congress selected George Washington of Virginia to lead the newly formed Continental army.

The congress then turned its attention to a navy. Stephen Hopkins of Rhode Island was the main supporter of creating a navy, and when the congress agreed with him in October 1775 it created the Continental navy. Hopkins's younger brother, Esek Hopkins, was put in charge of the navy. The army, meanwhile, was successful in getting the British to evacuate Boston on March 17, 1776. Many in the colonies took up the call for independence.

DECLARING INDEPENDENCE

As the calls for independence grew stronger throughout the colonies, Rhode Island decided to act first. After debate in the colonial assembly, on May 4, 1776, Rhode Island declared independence from the Crown. It was the first colony to take this action. The Rhode Island delegates to the Continental Congress supported the idea of all the colonies uniting and declaring independence. Finally, after much debate and some fear that a few colonies would

The Battle of Bunker Hill, on June 17, 1775, helped the colonists realize that they might have a chance at becoming independent from the British. *(Library of Congress)*

One of the boldest acts of the Second Continental Congress was to compose and sign the Declaration of Independence in summer 1776. *(National Archives, Old Military and Civil Records, NWCTB-360-ITEM1-ITEM1VOL3P94)*

The First Paragraph of the Declaration of Independence

Thomas Jefferson of Virginia is given credit as being the primary author of the Declaration of Independence. He began it with the following paragraph:

When in the Course of human events, it becomes necessary for one people to dissolve the political bands which have connected them with another, and to assume among the Powers of the earth, the separate and equal station to which the Laws of Nature and of Nature's God entitle them, a decent respect to the opinions of mankind requires that they should declare the causes which impel them to the separation.

not support independence, all 13 agreed on July 4, 1776, and the Declaration of Independence was adopted.

THE WAR IN RHODE ISLAND

From the start of the fighting in Massachusetts in 1775, Rhode Islanders joined their fellow Patriots in the fight for independence. Rhode Island soldiers fought in every major campaign of the war. The most famous Rhode Island soldier was Nathanael Greene, who was born in Warwick, Rhode Island. Greene became one of the heroes of the war, first as the leader of Rhode Island's militia and then as one of the primary generals in the Continental army.

At the beginning of the war, Captain Wallace and his British ships harassed the people of Rhode Island. The British raided the countryside for food and livestock and fired on a number of the towns in the colony. On December 8, 1776, Sir Henry Clinton moved into Newport with five British regiments and four Hessian units. The Hessians were hired soldiers from Germany. More than 450 residents of Aquidneck Island declared themselves loyal to the Crown. The occupation of Newport lasted for three years.

Nathanael Greene
(1742–1786)

Nathanael Greene was born in Warwick, Rhode Island, in 1742. He was brought up as a Quaker although he reportedly did not like the strict life his Quaker parents imposed on him. As a teenager, he was known to sneak out of his house to attend the dances and parties of his non-Quaker friends. In 1770, he moved to Coventry, Rhode Island, where his family owned an ironworks. From Coventry he was elected to the colonial assembly. As relations between the Crown and the colonies grew more strained, Greene felt that the colonies should prepare for the worst. In 1773, Greene was thrown out of the Society of Friends (who were pacifists) for going to Connecticut to talk about military preparations for the colonies.

In May 1775, Greene was appointed commanding general of the Rhode Island Army of Observation, and he took his troops to Boston to help General George Washington. In Boston, Greene was made a general in the Continental army and served throughout the war. Greene led forces in all of Washington's major campaigns. After Boston, he fought in New York, New Jersey, and Pennsylvania. When the war moved to the South, Greene was sent south to harass the British. He was with Washington when the British finally surrendered at Yorktown, Virginia. During the war, he also returned to Rhode Island to help lead the attempt to drive the British out of Newport. Greene's health was damaged in the war. He died in 1786 at the age of 43.

Nathanael Greene, in an engraving published in 1785, served as a general in the Continental army throughout the Revolutionary War. *(Library of Congress, Prints and Photographs Division [LC-USZ62-45338])*

Although there were numerous skirmishes between the Patriots and the British stationed in Newport, there was only one full-fledged battle fought in Rhode Island. It is known as the Battle of

Midway through the Revolutionary War, Sir Henry Clinton was appointed commander in chief of the British forces when General William Howe resigned. This engraving of Clinton was published between 1770 and 1780. *(Library of Congress, Prints and Photographs Division [LC-USZ62-45188])*

Rhode Island, and it took place on August 29, 1778. On February 6, 1778, the French officially joined the Americans in their war against British authority. The Battle of Rhode Island was supposed to be the first example of what the Americans could accomplish with the help of their new allies.

The plan was for American generals John Sullivan and Nathanael Greene to attack the British by crossing to the northern end of Aquidneck Island while the French fleet was to arrive by sea and then land its forces on the southern end of the island. When the French arrived off Rhode Island, the plan was put into motion. Comte d'Estaing was in charge of the French fleet, and when a British fleet came out from New York to engage him, he directed his ships out to sea to have room to maneuver. Before the two naval forces began their fight, the fleets were caught in a hurricane.

After the storm, the French decided that they needed to repair and refit their ships

Tories and Patriots

It has been estimated that at the beginning of the American Revolution the colonists were divided into three groups of almost equal size. The first group was the Patriots, who were in favor of the colonies becoming independent from Great Britain. These people supported the Continental Congress, the Declaration of Independence, and the Revolutionary War. The second group was known as Tories, and these were people who remained loyal to the Crown. As the Patriot forces prevailed, many Tories left the United States for Canada or England. The final group was neutral, supporting neither the Crown nor the Continental Congress. By the end of the war, most of the colonists supported the idea that the thirteen colonies should become one country.

The Battle of Rhode Island was the only Revolutionary War battle fought in the colony. In this undated drawing, Comte d'Estaing leads the French fleet into the Bay of Rhode Island to help support the colonial forces. *(Library of Congress, Prints and Photographs Division [LC-USZ62-95489])*

In August 1778, as shown in this 1779 etching, General John Sullivan's troops advance on the British in Newport at the Battle of Rhode Island. *(Library of Congress, Prints and Photographs Division [LC-USZ62-16834])*

before they would be ready to fight, and sailed off to Boston. This left the American forces to face the British in Newport alone. Many of the American militia members went home when they heard they were not going to be helped by the French. Sullivan and his 7,000 men fought a battle with the British ground forces on August 29, 1778. Although the Americans held their ground, Sul-

John Sullivan served as a Revolutionary War general, delegate to the First Continental Congress, and member of the Second Continental Congress, among other honors. *(Library of Congress, Prints and Photographs Division [LC-USZ62-39567])*

In a 1780s etching, the comte de Rochambeau leads French troops into Newport to help the colonists fight the British. Rochambeau led the French force that helped the colonial forces defeat the British at Yorktown. *(Library of Congress, Prints and Photographs Division [LC-USZ62-19422])*

livan worried that he would be trapped on the island by the British navy and was forced to withdraw. During the night of August 30, the Americans left the island. Had they stayed, they might have been overwhelmed as 5,000 British reinforcements arrived two days later.

Depicted in this painting by Charles Willson Peale, Jean-Baptiste-Donatien de Vimeur, comte de Rochambeau, commanded the French army during the Revolutionary War. *(Library of Congress, Prints and Photographs Division [LC-USZ62-121988])*

In October 1779, the British left Newport without a shot being fired. The British commanders wanted to strengthen their position in New York and recalled the forces that occupied Newport. For Rhode Island, the war was over. However, Rhode Island soldiers such as Greene continued to serve until the British surrendered at Yorktown, Virginia, on October 17, 1781. Without the help of the French, the outcome at Yorktown might have been different. Comte de Rochambeau arrived in Rhode Island with a large force in 1780. For almost a year, a British blockade kept him bottled up in Narragansett Bay. In June 1781, rather than run the blockade, Rochambeau marched his army south to Virginia to aid General Washington.

Throughout the long war, Rhode Island privateers harassed British shipping, making it hard for the British commanders to keep their troops well supplied in the field. Although the war was over, there was still much to do to make the former thirteen colonies into a single unified country, and Rhode Island would be at the center of the controversies.

8

Reluctant Member of the New Nation

At the end of the Revolutionary War, Rhode Island was in bad shape. Almost 4,000 Rhode Islanders died fighting in the war. In addition, many Loyalists left rather than be a part of the United States. In fact, between 1774 and 1782, the population of Rhode Island decreased by more than 10 percent. More than 900 homes in Rhode Island, 300 just in Newport, had been destroyed by the British as they bombarded the shores of Narragansett Bay and raided its farms and businesses to support their war efforts. At the same time, what did not get stolen by the British was often sent to the Rhode Island troops fighting throughout the colonies. Many of the ship owners and sailors in Rhode Island used their ships as privateers and to carry goods for the American troops.

With the war over, many merchants found themselves without cargoes for their ships. The Patriots in Rhode Island had abolished the slave trade in the colony in 1774. Those who obeyed the law no longer made the middle passage carrying slaves from Africa to the Caribbean. In addition, American ships were now banned from trading in any ports that were part of the British Empire. There was also a food shortage that would have caused a general famine if Connecticut had not sent food to the people of Rhode Island. All of these problems contributed to a general economic depression in Rhode Island and many other colonies after the war. Some in the colonies saw the problem as a result of the weaknesses of the Articles of Confederation.

ARTICLES OF CONFEDERATION

The First and Second Continental Congresses convened without any real legal authority to do so. The desire to pursue independence from Britain, the most powerful nation in the world at the time, forced the delegates to overlook some of the legalities of their situation. However, some in the Second Continental Congress felt that a more formal arrangement was needed. In 1776, the congress formed a committee to draft a plan for a national government. John Dickinson of Pennsylvania was appointed the chairman of the committee, and he quickly brought a proposal for a federal government before the congress.

Dickinson's plan called for a relatively strong central government. When the delegates to the congress began to debate the plan, it became obvious that they were not willing to accept a strong federal government. Many in the congress and throughout the colonies were reluctant to replace the dictatorial power of the Crown with a strong federal government. By the end of the debate, the congress came up with a plan for a federal government that would be able to pursue the war against the British but would have little power beyond that.

The plan they finally agreed on is known as the Articles of Confederation. It contains the first official mention of the former colonies as the United States of America. The delegates from Rhode Island had been among those who were most concerned about giving the federal government too much power. The Rhode Island Charter of 1664 was still the law of the land in the state. Under the charter, Rhode Island had enjoyed more liberty and independence than had any of the other colonies. The citizens of Rhode Island had no intention of giving any of that up to a federal government.

It took four years, until 1781, for all the states to pass the Articles of Confederation. One of the stumbling blocks to acceptance of the articles had been the claims some states had to lands west of the Appalachian Mountains. Some of the original colonial charters had granted lands from sea to sea without really knowing how much land that entailed. New York, Virginia, and some of the other colonies claimed large tracts of land. The smaller colonies, such as Rhode Island and Maryland, which had no western land claims, feared that if these states were allowed to grow into their western lands they would become big enough to overwhelm the small colonies.

The Articles of Confederation, shown here, were written by a committee of
the Continental Congress and intended as a constitution for the colonies.
(National Archives, National Archives Building, NWCTB-360-MISC-ROLL10F81)

Eventually, a compromise was reached and the large states gave up their claims to the west. The land between the Mississippi River and the Appalachian Mountains was ceded to the federal government for later development. Once that was done, the last holdout state, Maryland, ratified the Articles of Confederation in 1781. Almost immediately, the shortcomings of the articles began to create problems.

The federal government was not given the authority to levy taxes, and it had to depend on the states for the money needed to run the government. For the most part, states gave the federal government only a small portion of what it needed to operate and pay its debts from the war. The situation was such that many soldiers in the Continental army were not paid for serving during the war. In summer 1783, a large group of war veterans marched on the congress in Philadelphia demanding their back pay. The only solution that the federal government could come up with was to sneak out of town and establish a new capital in Trenton, New Jersey.

SOFT MONEY IN RHODE ISLAND

One of the greatest problems facing the states and the federal government was a lack of hard money. Gold and silver coins were considered hard money and had a real value in the new United States and around the world. Money was needed to rebuild or build new homes, farms, ships, factories, and public buildings. To make matters worse, the states and federal government had huge debts from the war. Rhode Island had borrowed heavily to support its troops in the war and to help outfit the many naval ships and privateers that sailed out of Narragansett Bay. Under the Articles of Confederation, Rhode Island could seek its own solutions to the financial crisis that faced the state.

In many states, such as Massachusetts, political power was held by the wealthy merchant class who had loaned the state money. To ensure that they got what was coming to them, Massachusetts demanded that all the state taxes be paid in hard money. In Rhode Island, on the other hand, a group known as the Country Party gained political control of the state under the leadership of Jonathan J. Hazard. Hazard and his followers came up with a plan that was more likely to help the farmers and small merchants of the state. The Country Party voted to have the state issue paper currency that could be used to pay taxes and debts. Paper money was referred to as soft money, in part because it was made of paper, and because it had no real value.

The paper money of Rhode Island caused numerous problems and upset many who had loaned the state money during the war. However, it was good for average people in Rhode Island since

Samuel Slater's construction of mills, or spinning machines powered by water, is considered to be the beginning of the Industrial Revolution in America. He built Slater Mill (shown here) in Pawtucket, Rhode Island, in 1793. *(Library of Congress, Prints and Photographs Division [HAER, RI,4-PAWT,3-8])*

The Birth of the Textile Industry in the United States

In England, new machines had been devised that used water power to spin large amounts of thread for making cloth. The manufactured cloth that could then be produced was one of the mainstays of British trade around the world. To maintain the British monopoly on manufactured cloth, the British made it a crime to sell any of the machinery outside of England. They also refused to allow anyone who knew about the machines to leave the country. In the United States, those who could not afford British cloth wore clothes made of coarse material made by hand spinning and weaving.

In 1789, Moses Brown tried to turn the farm craft of weaving into a manufacturing process, and he set up a factory in Pawtucket, Rhode Island, to spin and make cloth. But without the machinery the English used, he was unable to mechanize the process. At about same time, Samuel Slater arrived in New York. He had worked for the people who had developed the spinning machines in England, and it is believed that he left England claiming to be a farmer.

Slater soon found his way to Pawtucket and built spinning machines powered by water that were like those he had helped build in England. The company that Brown created using Slater's spinning frames was soon successfully making yarn for the growing textile industry in New England. Many consider Slater's mill the start of the Industrial Revolution in America.

This engraving of Pawtucket, Rhode Island, was published in an 1836 memoir of Samuel Slater. *(Library of Congress, Prints and Photographs Division [LC-USZ62-87182])*

paper money allowed them to pay their taxes and rebuild their lives. It meant that Rhode Island avoided many of the problems that other states faced. In Massachusetts, farmers in the western part of the state organized and started a revolt against the government that was controlled by the wealthy merchants in the eastern part of the state. Daniel Shays was the leader of this revolt, known as Shays's Rebellion.

Rhode Island was dealing with its problems, and its merchants were finding new markets around the world outside the British Empire. Rhode Island was also at the forefront of the Industrial Revolution, which would sweep the country in the 19th century. However, many in other states were dissatisfied with the situation under the Articles of Confederation. Maryland and Virginia faced a conflict over control of Chesapeake Bay. New Jersey and Connecticut were angry with New York for trying to monopolize trade in the area. Other states also experienced problems similar to Shays's Rebellion in Massachusetts. Many feared that the United States would not survive for very long if the situation did not change.

THE CONSTITUTIONAL CONVENTION, 1787

In 1786, Virginia invited all the states to send delegates to a convention in Annapolis, Maryland, which was one of the many places that served as the national capital during this period. Some people hoped that the Annapolis convention could work out some of the problems between the states and suggest changes to the Articles of Confederation. Only five states—Delaware, New Jersey, New York, Pennsylvania, and Virginia—sent representatives. Since any changes to the articles required unanimous approval, there was little those who attended could hope to accomplish. The group thought the articles needed a major overhaul and suggested that a convention be held in Philadelphia the following year.

When the convention to amend the Articles of Confederation met in May 1787 in Philadelphia, it immediately faced a number of problems. First and foremost was the need for agreement from all 13 states to change the articles. Rhode Island, which feared the loss of its independence, refused to send delegates to the convention. In addition, many felt that the articles were too flawed to fix. They wanted to throw them out completely.

Looking back, the convention probably had no authority to do what it did, but that did not stop the delegates from drawing up a new set of procedures and writing a new constitution for the United States. Under the new procedures, each delegation was given one vote, and it would take a majority of the delegations present to pass anything that came before the convention. In addition, they agreed that the new constitution would replace the Articles of Confederation when nine states had ratified it. These rules made it impossible for one or two states to prevent the majority from going forward.

During the process of writing the constitution, there were a number of hurdles that the states had to overcome. One of the biggest was how the federal legislature would work. The large states wanted representation based on population size. The small states wanted each state to have equal representation. Finally a compromise was reached and a federal congress was created with two houses. The Senate was to have two senators from each state, while representation in the House

Shays's Rebellion

Daniel Shays and many of his farmer neighbors in western Massachusetts found themselves in jeopardy of losing their farms as they were hauled into court and forced to pay their taxes and other debts. The problem was that the state would take only hard money in payment and there was little or no gold and silver coin in the pockets of Massachusetts farmers. In protest, Shays and his followers forced courts to close. They then turned their attention to the arsenal in Springfield, Massachusetts, where the state had a large supply of weapons.

Fearing the rebellion would spread, Massachusetts sent 600 militia from the eastern part of the state to defend the arsenal. When Shays arrived on January 25, 1787, with 2,000 followers, the militia feared being overwhelmed by the large crowd. The militia leader, General William Shepard, ordered his troops to fire their cannons into the crowd. Four were killed and more than 20 were wounded. During the next few weeks, the militia fought a number of skirmishes with the rebels. Daniel Shays and some of the other leaders of the rebellion fled the state. They first went to Rhode Island, where they were told they were not welcome. They then went to Vermont. The fact that the federal government had no ability under the Articles of Confederation to come to the aid of Massachusetts gave fuel to the argument that a better arrangement of federal authority was needed.

of Representatives would be based on population. This system has worked well and continues without change today.

The new U.S. Constitution was passed by the Constitutional Convention on September 17, 1787. It was

> PENNSYLVANIA, ſſ.
>
> By the *Preſident* and the *Supreme Ex*
> *ecutive Council* of the Common-
> wealth of *Pennſylvania*,
> A PROCLAMATION.
>
> WHEREAS the General Aſſembly of this Common-
> wealth, by a law entituled 'An act for co-operating with
> " the ſtate of Maſſachuſetts bay, agreeable to the articles of
> " confederation, in the apprehending of the proclaimed rebels
> " DANIEL SHAYS, LUKE DAY, ADAM WHEELER
> " and ELI PARSONS," have enacted, " that rewards ad-
> " ditional to thoſe offered and promiſed to be paid by the ſtate
> " of Maſſachuſetts Bay, for the apprehending the aforeſaid
> " rebels, be offered by this ſtate ;" WE do hereby offer the
> following rewards to any perſon or perſons who ſhall, within
> the limits of this ſtate, apprehend the rebels aforeſaid, and
> ecure them in the gaol of the city and county of Philadelphia,
> ---- viz. For the apprehending of the ſaid Daniel Shays, and
> ſecuring him as aforeſaid, the reward of *One hundred and Fifty*
> *Pounds* lawful money of the ſtate of Maſſachuſetts Bay, and
> *One Hundred Pounds* lawful money of this ſtate ; and for the
> apprehending the ſaid Luke Day, Adam Wheeler and Eli
> Parſons, and ſecuring them as aforeſaid, the reward (reſpec-
> tively) of *One Hundred Pounds* lawful money of Maſſachuſetts
> Bay and *Fifty Pounds* lawful money of this ſtate : And all
> judges, juſtices, ſheriffs and conſtables are hereby ſtrictly en-
> joined and required to make diligent ſearch and enquiry after,
> and to uſe their utmoſt endeavours to apprehend and ſecure the
> ſaid Daniel Shays, Luke Day, Adam Wheeler and Eli Par-
> ſons, their aiders, abettors and comforters, and every of them,
> ſo that they may be dealt with according to law.
>
> > GIVEN in Council, under the hand of the Preſident, and
> > the Seal of the State, at Philadelphia, this tenth
> > day of March, in the year of our Lord one thouſand
> > ſeven hundred and eighty-ſeven.
> > > BENJAMIN FRANKLIN.
> > ATTEST
> > > JOHN ARMSTRONG, jun. Secretary.

This proclamation by the state of Pennsylvania offers a reward for Daniel Shays and three other people who participated in Shays's Rebellion. *(Library of Congress, Prints and Photographs Division [LC-USZ62-77992])*

then sent to the states for ratification. It would replace the Articles of Confederation when nine states had ratified it. It was almost three years before Rhode Island agreed to accept the new constitution.

On September 17, 1787, the Constitution was passed by the Constitutional Convention. The only step that remained to make it the governing document of the United States was for nine colonies to ratify it. *(National Archives)*

RATIFYING THE CONSTITUTION

The second smallest state, Delaware, became the first state to ratify the Constitution on December 7, 1787. New Hampshire holds the distinction of being the ninth state to ratify, which made the new constitution the law of the land. Once New Hampshire had become the ninth state, it seemed like the others would go along so they would remain a part of the United States. Two of the holdouts, New York and Virginia, voted to ratify shortly after New Hampshire. North Carolina was concerned about the lack of specific rights being included in the Constitution. When the North Carolina delegates were promised that a Bill of Rights would be added, they voted late in 1789, becoming the 12th state to ratify.

Rhode Island was then the only state that had not accepted the new federal government. This upset many people, including the new president, George Washington. When he toured the colonies after his election in 1789, he skipped Rhode Island even though he toured the other New England states and nearby New York City was the national capital at the time. The new federal government threatened a variety of actions against Rhode Island if it did not join the union.

The Country Party was not yet ready to give up Rhode Island's independence. The party members wanted to be sure that they had taken care of the majority of the state's debts before they would give up their own paper money. The leaders of the Country Party did such a good job of convincing the people of Rhode Island that the new Constitution was not in Rhode Island's best interest that they repeatedly voted against it.

For the people of the state, there were a number of reasons to vote against the Constitution. Some were concerned that their rights were not protected by the Constitution. Rhode Island sent a list of 18 specific rights to Congress, and most of them were incorporated into the Bill of Rights, which was added to the Constitution on November 3, 1791. Others, especially the Quakers in the state, objected because the Constitution allowed for the importation of slaves to continue until 1808. Still others saw an independent Rhode Island becoming a flourishing trading center without interference from the federal authorities.

Those who wanted the state to ratify the Constitution spread rumors to persuade the voters. One rumor was that if Rhode Island did not ratify the Constitution, the state would be split up between Connecticut and Massachusetts. Another rumor went around that Providence was going to secede from Rhode Island and join the United States on its own. Although neither rumor was true, they show how divided the state was over the Constitution.

Between 1787 and 1789, Rhode Island held 13 different conventions where the people of the state were given the opportunity to vote on the federal Constitution. In all 13 instances, the people voted against the Constitution. By 1790, the leaders of the Country Party felt they had accomplished all they could with their monetary policy and were ready to accept the new Constitution. However, they had done too good a job of turning the majority of the people in the state against ratification. The only chance they had was to hold a convention where the communities of the state would send representatives.

In March 1790, a representative convention met in South Kingston, Rhode Island, to vote on the federal Constitution. It quickly became apparent from the arguments that were taking place that this group would vote down the Constitution. Rather than provoke the federal government, which was now threatening sanctions against Rhode Island, the convention was adjourned. It reconvened in May 1790 in Newport. Between the two meetings, sentiment had shifted enough that on May 29, 1790, the members of the Rhode Island convention voted 34 to 32 to accept the Constitution, and Rhode Island reluctantly became the 13th state.

Shown in a well-known painting by Gilbert Stuart, George Washington was the first president of the United States. When he toured the colonies in 1789, he did not visit Rhode Island because it was the only state that had not ratified the Constitution. *(Library of Congress, Prints and Photographs Division [LC-USZ62-117116])*

President Washington was so relieved that the crisis with Rhode Island had ended that he and Secretary of State Thomas Jefferson, along with a number of government officials, made a special trip to Newport in August 1790. In the end, the people of Newport showed they were glad to be a part of the United States. Large crowds turned out to see President Washington and the other dignitaries who traveled with him. The town turned the event into a celebration with the ringing of bells and the firing of cannons. Rhode Island, which had started out as a haven for Roger Williams and others seeking freedom, had shown its independence throughout its history and in the end took its rightful place as one of the 13 original United States.

Rhode Island Time Line

1524

★ Giovanni da Verrazano visits Narragansett Bay and Block Island.

1614

★ Adriaen Block explores coastal Rhode Island and Block Island.

1635

★ William Blackstone settles in Valley Falls.

1636

★ Roger Williams founds Providence.

1638

★ Williams and 12 others establish the Proprietors' Company for Providence Plantation.
★ A group including Anne Hutchinson, John Clarke, and William Coddington leave Massachusetts seeking religious freedom and go to Aquidneck Island, in Rhode Island.

1639

★ Coddington and his group establish a separate settlement, Newport, at the southern end of Aquidneck Island.

1642

★ Shawomet, a fourth settlement, is founded by Samuel Gorton.

1643

★ After being convicted of blasphemy, Gorton goes to England and receives protection from a parliamentary commission headed by the earl of Warwick.

1644

★ Williams receives a charter from Parliament, and Providence, Newport, Portsmouth, and Warwick (Shawomet) merge and become Providence Plantations.

1647

★ Representatives from Warwick attend the first recorded general assembly of the colony in 1647.

1648

★ Gorton returns to the colony and renames his settlement Warwick in honor of the earl who helped him.

1651

★ William Coddington obtains a charter that establishes the Aquidneck colony, and Williams and John Clarke go to England to protest it.

1652

★ The Aquidneck colony charter is revoked.

1654

★ The colony is reunited.

1660

★ Charles II becomes king of England at the end of civil war.

1663

★ Rhode Island and Providence Plantations are established by royal charter by Charles II.

1675

★ **December:** During King Philip's War, colonists attack the neutral Narragansett in the Great Swamp massacre, near West Kingston, Rhode Island.

1676

★ **March 26:** Narragansett leader Canonchet kills 65 settlers and 20 Native Americans led by Captain Michael Pierce.
★ **March 29:** The Narragansett attack Providence, burning many buildings.
★ **August:** King Philip (Metacomet) is killed, ending King Philip's War.

1764

★ Sugar Act (Revenue Act of 1764) restricts the sugar and molasses trade.

1772

★ Rhode Island's John Brown and other colonists burn the *Gaspee,* a British customs ship.

1776

★ **May 4:** Rhode Island's General Assembly is the first to vote to end allegiance to the king of England.

- ★ **July 18:** Rhode Island's General Assembly ratifies the Declaration of Independence.
- ★ **December:** The British capture Aquidneck Island and occupy Newport until October 1779.

1778

- ★ The British successfully maintain control against a combined American and French attack.
- ★ **August 29:** In the Battle of Rhode Island, the British counterattack and are defeated.

1779

- ★ **October:** The British withdraw their troops from Newport.

1780–81

- ★ Newport is home to Comte de Rochambeau and a large French army.

1787

- ★ Rhode Island does not send delegates to the Constitutional Convention.

1790

- ★ **May 29:** Rhode Island is the last to ratify the U.S. Constitution.

Rhode Island Historical Sites

EAST GREENWICH

Varnum House Museum   Varnum House was built by James Mitchell Varnum in 1773. Varnum was a lawyer, a general in the Rhode Island militia, and a delegate to the Second Continental Congress. It is open to the public.

> *Address:* 57 Pierce Street, East Greenwich,
>   Rhode Island 02818
> *Phone:* 401-884-1776

JOHNSTON

Clemence-Irons House   Richard Clemence, an early settler, built this house around 1680, making it one of the oldest houses in Rhode Island.

> *Address:* 38 George Waterman Road, Johnston,
>   Rhode Island 02919
> *Phone:* 617-227-3956
> *Web Site:* www.spnea.org/visit/homes/clemence/htm

LINCOLN

Arnold House   The Arnold House was built in 1693 by Eleazor Arnold, an early settler. It is one of few existing examples of "stone ender" architecture, where one end of the building that includes the chimney is made of stone.

> *Address:* 487 Great Road, Lincoln,
>   Rhode Island 02865
> *Phone:* 617-227-3956
> *Web Site:* www.spnea.org/visit/homes/arnold.htm

NEWPORT

Great Friends Meeting House   Built in 1699, the Great Friends Meeting House is the oldest house of worship in Newport.

> *Address:* Farewell & Marlborough Street, Newport,
>   Rhode Island 02840
> *Phone:* 401-846-0813
> *Web Site:* www.newporthistorical.org

Hunter House   Hunter House was started in 1748 by Jonathon Nichols, Jr., a prosperous merchant and colonial official, and is an outstanding example of Georgian colonial architecture.

> *Address:* 54 Washington Street, Newport,
>   Rhode Island 02840
> *Phone:* 401-847-1000
> *Web Site:* www.newportmansions.org/page3551.cfm

Seven Day Baptist Meeting House   The Seven Day Baptists built their very simple meeting house plan church in 1730.

> *Address:* 82 Touro Street, Newport,
>   Rhode Island 02840
> *Phone:* 401-846-0813
> *Web Site:* www.newporthistorical.org/the.htm

Touro Synagogue   Touro Synagogue was designed by Peter Harrison, dedicated in 1763, and continues today as the oldest synagogue in America.

> *Address:* Touro Street, Newport,
>   Rhode Island 02840

Phone: 401-847-4794

Web Site: www.tourosynagogue.org

Wanton-Lyman-Hazard House Built for Stephen Mumford in the 1670s, the Wanton-Lyman-Hazard House is the oldest house in Newport.

Address: 17 Broadway, Newport,
  Rhode Island 02840
Phone: 401-846-0813
Web Site: www.newporthistorical.org

PROVIDENCE

John Brown House John and Sarah Brown moved into this house in 1788, which is an example of Georgian brick architecture. John Brown was known for his participation in the burning of the *Gaspee* in 1772.

Address: 52 Power Street, Providence,
  Rhode Island 02906
Phone: 401-331-8575
Web Site: www.rihs.org/John%20Brown%20House.htm

Meeting House, First Baptist Church The Meeting House was built in 1774–75 and is the first Baptist church with a steeple erected in America.

Address: 75 North Main Street, Providence,
  Rhode Island 20903
Phone: 401-454-3418
Web Site: www.tourprovidence.com/visitors/attractions.
  cfm

SAUNDERSTOWN

Casey Farm The Casey Farm, which dates from the mid-18th century, is on Narragansett Bay.

Address: 2325 Boston Neck Road, Saunderstown,
Rhode Island 02874

Phone: 401-295-1030

Web Site: www.spnea.org/visit/homes/casey.htm

Further Reading

BOOKS

Beals, Carleton. *Colonial Rhode Island.* Camden, N.J.: Nelson, 1970.

Fradin, Dennis B. *The Rhode Island Colony.* Chicago: Children's Press, 1989.

James, Sydney V. *Colonial Rhode Island: A History.* New York: Scribner's, 1975.

Kling, Andrew A. *Rhode Island.* San Diego: Lucent, 2002.

Warner, J. F. *Rhode Island.* Minneapolis, Minn.: Lerner Publishing Group, 2002.

WEB SITES

The Official Rhode Island Tourism Web Site. "History & Famous Rhode Islanders." Available online. URL: visitrhodeisland.com/history/famous.html. Downloaded on May 16, 2004.

Rhode Island General Assembly. "Rhode Island History." Available online. URL: www.rilin.state.ri.us/studteaguide/RhodeIsland-History/rodehist.html. Downloaded on May 16, 2004.

Rhode Island USGenWeb Project. "Rhode Island History. A Short History of Rhode Island." Available online. URL: www.rootsweb.com/~rigenweb/history.html. Downloaded on May 16, 2004.

Index

Page numbers in *italic* indicate photographs. Page numbers in **boldface** indicate box features. Page numbers followed by m indicate maps. Page numbers followed by c indicate time line entries. Page numbers followed by t indicate tables or graphs.